The Guide to Easy
WOOD FLOOR
Care & Maintenance

A Complete Owner's Manual for Hardwood Floors
by Grant Aslett

To get a FREE newsletter and catalog of all Don Aslett's books (quantity discounts), products, speaking information and seminar availability SEND A POSTCARD with your name and address to

Don Aslett's Cleaning Center
PO Box 700
Pocatello, ID 83204
888-748-3535

The Guide to Easy Wood Floor Care
 Published by Marsh Creek Press, PO Box 700, Pocatello ID 83204.

ISBN 1-880759-00-4

Illustrator: Kerry Otteson
Editor: Carol Cartaino
Production: Heidi Payne

Acknowledgments:

Thanks to all who gave me ideas and input, especially my father, Don Aslett and Jon Bell of Bell Hardwood floors. A big thank you also to the manufacturers of quality wood flooring products!

Table of Contents

Wood Floor Owners:
No Longer Out on a Limb?

The wood floor question is a big one, with nowhere to get answers, as you already know, because you bought this book. I've been involved in the maintenance field for more than twenty years, working with my dad, Don Aslett, "America's #1 Cleaning Expert," cleaning everything from carpets to toilets to hardwood floors. Our cleaning organization gets national exposure through our cleaning books and national programs on both television and radio. We also have a mail-order company that makes professional cleaning supplies available to consumers across the country. When Oprah the Home Show, or Regis and Kathie Lee need solid cleaning information, they call us.

Don and I have spent many hours researching and resolving cleaning problems together. We can quickly give answers to cleaning questions about hard water deposits or no-wax floors, but wood care is a little more involved.

So we decided the subject deserved a book all its own. We decided to put my name on the book because I've had more recent hands-on practical experience with wood flooring, but this is a combination of our knowledge and many years of experience and research.

The time has come!

Wood floors are great, we love them! But no one will tell us how to maintain them, what to do and when. Nobody, including the wood floor industry itself, has come out with clear and practical answers to the simple question, "How can I care for my hardwood floor?" On one hand you have the manufacturers and retailers. They are selling new floors, so they don't want to hint that wood needs special care. At the other extreme are the installers and refinishers—their solution to every question is "sand and refinish." Needless to say, that leaves a big black hole in between, so no wonder 90% of all wood floor owners are in the dark.

This book addresses that big gap in information for wood floor owners and judging from the thousands of questions we get, it is needed!!! I'll be honest with you, this book will come up against the advice of some wood floor people, but it will give practical solutions to the most common problems wood floor owners come up against. It will also explain how to maintain wood floors properly and how to obtain the best-looking floor possible, as well as when to seek advice from a specialist. Our goal is to get to the bottom line and enable you to solve your wood care problems. We all love wood floors! And once you learn how to take care of them you will fall in love all over again!

An important note about our credentials now:

We don't claim to be the final word on the subject, but a practical guide. Our information and research comes from hands-on experience cleaning, repairing, selling, refinishing, and—equally important—owning of wood floors. We have been in all of these situations again and again.

Follow the information in this book and it will assist you in making the right decisions and enable you to fully enjoy your wood floors—at last!

Grant Aslett

FINISHED WOOD FLOOR

4

Chapter One

First Things First, Where Do You Stand?

Where are YOU in the Wood Floor Maze?

We are interested in wood floor ownership because of the beauty, prestige, and warmth of wood. Wood floors are a great sales feature in a home, and wood is now the number one preferred flooring choice, but the thought of maintaining them often changes people's mind. I have yet to hear someone say, "I'm getting a wood floor because it is so easy to take care of." Shopping for flooring, we become hypnotized by that beautiful grain pattern. We often don't realize the maintenance involved until we've lived on the floor for a month or two. Then we feel deserted by the installer, retailer, or contractor with nowhere to turn.

Here's the scoop, up front, so you can make the right choice for you. Or to rid you of that deserted feeling if you're stuck. I have owned three different wood floors and had the opportunity to help with the wood floors of numerous friends and family members, not to mention all the professional work I've done on wood floors.

EXISTING WOOD FLOORS

My first apartment had wood floors. When I moved in the floors needed attention, but they weren't mine to decide their destiny. Very few rentals will have wood floors because of the stigma that they are a maintenance nightmare. Most landlords will cover them up with carpet. They can get a carpet cleaned and often include it in the cost of the rental agreement. Dealing with a trashed wood floor is not so inexpensive or simple.

I came across my second floor when I purchased an older home with ugly brown carpet. This was our starter home and it was cheap, a real fixer-upper. We really felt we'd gotten our money's worth when we peeled up that ugly carpet and found oak floors that no one knew were underneath there.

Countless people buy a home with existing wood floors. Most of the calls I receive on wood floors are from people who discover wood floors in older homes.

Wood floors were very popular in the twenties through the forties. In fact for a period of time, hardwood floors were required in new homes in order to get an FHA or VA loan on them. A solid wood floor in many cases proved to be more economical to put down than other types of floors (the cost of wood was very reasonable back then). When wall-to-wall carpeting came in strong, people flocked to the carpet stores to cover up their wood floors, because of the continual maintenance—those floors never seemed to stay clean and waxed and the owners lived in constant fear of water or other damage. A contractor told me that they used to schedule the carpet layer a day after they put the final coat of finish on a wood

floor, and the "high maintenance" reputation of wood floors was almost always the reason.

Now, a new generation of homeowners peek under the corner of their carpets (as I did with my ugly carpet) to find a hardwood floor. It looks good and they shiver with delight thinking, "I've always wanted a wood floor." It is great when you own the home, and what to do with that floor is all up to you, but where do you go for help?

NEW WOOD FLOORS

I recently sold my fixer-upper and bought a beautiful new home with brand spanking new wood floors.

Today, wood is a popular choice for new homes and remodeling projects. Americans are installing wood flooring at the fastest pace ever, but the high cost of wood today is making us more concerned than ever before about the right maintenance for them. Wood floors aren't used as a subfloor any more.

When I moved into my new home, I had a stack of manuals for the dishwasher, the range, the garage door opener, and the hinges on the cupboard hardware. I had repair, care, and maintenance information on the faucets, the furnace, and even the carpet. I even know what paint is on the walls, but on the wood floor—zilch. In all of my wood floor experience, I have yet to hear of a wood floor coming with directions or an owner's manual. That's where this book comes in. It will be your owner's manual for wood flooring… new… old… or in between.

NOW YOU NEED TO BECOME "Dr. Wood"

Now that we have joined the wood floor owners and are committed to these floors, no matter how we happened upon them, we need to become "Dr. Wood." We need to take the time to stop and diagnose where we stand with our wood floor and from that diagnosis we can prescribe a remedy. Have you ever tried to just call the doctor and get medical advice? No, they need to poke, push, peek in your ears, and take pulse and temperature before they offer a solution. It is the same with your floor. Every day people call wanting a quick fix to their wood floor pains. I give them the best solution I can, after asking a bunch of questions, but nothing takes the place of poking, looking at, and feeling the floor itself. That is how you are going to diagnose your floor. Only after we've diagnosed the situation can we keep our floor beautiful (the way it should be) and relatively maintenance free! So carry on, "Dr. Wood."

Determining the overall condition of a wood floor is the first step. This will help us determine how we are going to proceed—whether it needs a simple cleaning, a maintenance coat of finish, a light sanding, or a complete resurfacing.

How to Make Your Floor Easy to Maintain!

When you inherit a wood floor don't worry too much about what kind of wood it is, whether it's good old red oak, Brazilian cherry wood, Indonesian or Idaho sagebrush. The fact is it's there, and we treat it almost all the same when it comes to repair and maintenance. Our concern is **HOW TO TAKE CARE OF IT**.

When you start to look closely at wood floors you will discover many designs: standard 2 1/4" wide solid, 3/4" tongue and groove, parquet floors (made of small pieces of wood laid together in

squares); plank floors (5"-6" wide); you'll find some floors with dowels for looks, and some have recessed or beveled edges. Again, if the floor is already there don't worry about the details or defining its origin.

WOOD CONDITION

First, we are going to judge the condition of the **wood itself** *ONLY*. Look for gouges, cuts, scars, and nail holes from carpet tack strips. Cracks and warped boards are also a problem.

Don't confuse the condition of the finish with the condition of the wood. Look past the finish for the moment and focus on the wood alone. It is possible for the wood to be in perfect shape while the finish is totally shot.

Give the wood a rating from one to five. A "one" rating meaning it doesn't look salvageable, because of all the heavy damage, warping, and wear. Three would mean the overall appearance is fair, despite several cracks, and nicks, etc. Five would be brand new with no damage at all to the wood itself. See chart on page 15.

We also need to determine if the floor has been sanded before. In the old days when the finish got bad, the school gym floor, church floor, or dance floor was immediately sanded and recoated. Church groups were famous for getting the members together every couple of years to sand the gymnasium. These floors were often over-sanded and required replacement after only a few years. Since then we have learned that we can maintain a wood floor almost indefinitely without sanding, if proper care is taken of it.

Inspect the edges, and see if there are any differences in the level of the floor. Sometimes it is necessary to pull off the baseboard to get a good reading. **This is important!** Good solid wood floors can withstand up to ten sandings, but some of the new engineered or parquet floors can only handle one or two light sandings. Getting access to a side view of the wood can help determine if the floor is solid or engineered and how much more sanding can safely be done. Most of the old existing floors are solid wood. Today's floors are a combination.

Laminated vs. Engineered

Not long ago we referred to non-solid wood floors as "laminated" because they were constructed of plywood and other wood with a 3/16" thick wood surface laminated to the top. With the introduction of melamine laminates (Pergo) flooring it gets confusing. So in the wood floor industry when referring to laminates they mean the Pergo-type floors. And the new term for non-solid wood floors is engineered multi-ply wood flooring.

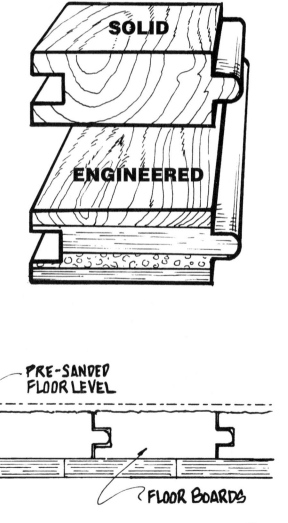

SOLID

ENGINEERED

WALL

PRE-SANDED FLOOR LEVEL

SUB WALL

SUB-FLOOR

FLOOR BOARDS

9

Other Wood Considerations

How sound is the floor? Squeaks and groans are hard to track down and repair. So if they are minor, don't worry. If it sounds like the house is alive when you walk across it, then the floor needs some professional attention. There are some remodel and fix-it books that can help you tighten up and eliminate squeaks.

Are there spots from pet accidents? Are there burns from cigarettes, stray coals from fireplaces, or a dropped frying pan? Is there damage from insects such as termites that might be apparent? Are there only a few areas with spot damage that need to be repaired? Does the entire floor rate high except for one spot near the window that was exposed to too many open windows during rainstorms? Or

---

The word "FINISH":
Almost everyone has a different understanding when we use the word "finish." The wood floor installer instantly thinks of the polyurethane product he puts on the floor. The maintenance guy thinks of the acrylic polish (wax) he applies to the supermarket floor. So for our purposes here in this book, the "finishes" we refer to are permanent wood floor finishes such as an oil-or water-base polyurethane. When we refer to the floor maintenance products we will use the words "acrylic polish (wax)." However, when you go to the store, "wax" will be called "floor finish."

---

holes in the floor from old steam radiators? It might be in great shape except for one board that is cracked and shedding slivers.

Remember, we are only judging the type and condition of the wood itself. Use the chart on page 16 for quick grading of the floor. We will focus on the finish next.

FINISH CONDITION

Next we need to determine the condition of the finish, as well as what kind it is. The finish, too, we will give a rating. *The condition of the finish is often related to the condition of the wood, for instance, there might be deep chips or dents in the floor that go through the finish and into the wood, but let's concentrate on just the finish for a bit.*

A "one" rating would be no finish (bare wood) or extremely chipped and scratched finish. Three is not an eyesore, but it needs attention. And a five would mean the floor needs little or no attention. See the chart on page 16 and use the simple test on the next page to help determine the condition of the finish. Old varnishes often yellow and turn very dark. A floor you have removed the carpet from might have a nice glossy finish, but because of age that finish has yellowed or turned dark and is not acceptable.

REMEMBER!

We are grading the FINISH, not the wood, so look at the surface. Use this test then refer to chart on page 16 for easy grading.

Here is a simple test for Finish Assessment

Pick a spot that is an average sample of the entire floor. The edges and corners of the floor might have a good coat of seal left on them still, but in the traffic areas most of the finish has worn away. It is important to find an average sample of the floor to use for this experiment.

Get a cup of water and pour a tablespoon or two onto the sample area, and observe what happens.

Scenario One

If the water soaks in right away and leaves a darkened spot on the wood, that means the wood has little or no seal. Caution should be taken here, because any water can damage the wood rather quickly. (According to the chart on page 16, this floor would rate a one or two.

Scenario Two

If you put the test drop on the wood and it doesn't seem to soak in, let it sit there for a few minutes. After a few minutes, if it has partially soaked in or you notice a slight change in wood color, the chances are your wood has been sealed at some time but is not 100% protected now. The finish is partially worn off or it is an oil seal. The rating for this floor is a three or four.

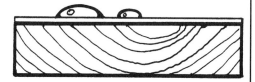

Scenario Three

If the water sits on top like it is on glass at first, and when you come back a few minutes later it is still there, and there has been no darkening of the wood, the surface has probably been sealed with a good permanent seal, and it is still intact. This floor rates a five.

IMPORTANT NOTE: A good waxed surface will and can perform about the same as a permanent seal in these tests.

TYPE OF FINISH

This may be the most difficult to determine, but we are going to do the best we can. It is not absolutely critical to know the specific brand name of the finish and what year it was put down. Don't be discouraged if you follow all these directions and simply get an idea.

The first step is to ask! You never know, someone might already have the information you need, or who knows, there might just be a half-used can of wood floor finish left in the garage. In a new home ask the contractor, he will refer you to the wood floor installer. My wood floor is in the kitchen. I assumed it was finished with polyurethane, but I wasn't sure until I tracked down the installer and asked.

The first thing we need to determine is if the finish is permanent or not. Gym floors are famous for having a very durable resinous finish, often high gloss. On the other hand, in many older homes penetrating oils or paste wax were used as finish on the floors. Oil and paste wax usually has a satin or dull finish.

Run your hand across the surface of the floor, if you can feel the grain, it is probably not a permanent finish, or it is a very thin coat.

Permanent finishes include any seal that is **solvent-based** such as **varnish, lacquer,** and even some **shellacs.** Nowadays, these permanent finishes are urethanes, which may be either solvent- or water-based.

12

TEST

If the floor appears to have a clear finish over the wood, it might be a water-base acrylic polish (wax). Test it with some wax stripper or a dose of ammonia. If the surface turns white and softens rather quickly we know it's a removable acrylic polish (wax). It could also be a paste wax which is removed the same way.

Another way to test without using any solution is to grab a pocket knife and scrape the surface. A permanent finish tends to scar. An acrylic polish (wax) will flake and powder off.

Get some paint remover, you can buy a small container at a paint or hardware store. Test by spreading a small amount in an inconspicuous area—under the couch, in a closet, or where the entertainment center sits. Let this sit for three to five minutes, or follow the label directions. If the finish bubbles up it is most likely a solvent-base resinous finish. Also notice how thick the finish is. If there is a big buildup, where it looks like several coats have been applied, it will affect our refinishing decision later.

When I bought my first home, the fixer-upper, I peeled up the carpet and found a nice solid oak floor. I knew I was going to do some major remodeling in the next two years, rip down the old lathe and plaster walls, rewire, insulate and re-sheetrock, so I didn't want to refinish my floor until that time. I cleaned the floor well and put three coats of a professional acrylic polish (wax) on it. This gave me a high-gloss look, much like a permanent finish. If someone moved in after me, it would have been hard for them to determine what kind of finish my floor had on it without using these simple tests.

Again, it is very important to know if the floor has an acrylic polish (wax) on it. Wax can wreak havoc when we get ready to apply permanent finish if the right steps are not taken to prepare the floor. We will discuss wax stripping later in Chapter Seven, that is why we determine whether we have acrylic polish (wax) or permanent finish. **You can't put perma-**

nent finish over the top of acrylic polish (wax) or it will peel up in sheets.

Sometimes a floor will be a combination of several types of finishes, waxes, polishes, cleaners, etc., and there is no way to research its exact genealogy. In this case we will want to sand the floor completely. If you get stumped and can't figure out what is on your floor, don't lose sleep over it, most any floor can be dealt with.

PENETRATING OIL

Danish/Tung

Many old floors were finished or I should say "treated" with penetrating oil products. These would penetrate the wood and keep water from getting in as well as keep it from drying out and cracking. Oil-treated floors were maintained with a paste wax every month or two, it was the only way to keep them looking good. This didn't give a protection like the old varnishes, but did create a rich wood look.

Oil finishes are rarely part of wood floor care today, because of the high maintenance involved. Oil finishes offer the least amount of protection to a floor and this is where the big fear of water comes from. Oiled floors are more susceptible to water penetrating the surface and between the boards. These oil-treated floors were so hard to take care of, the owners were thrilled to be able to cover them up with carpet.

A good test for an oil finish is to get a heavy duty cleaner or wax stripper and clean a small area. If this seems to dry out the wood it is probably some type of oil and paste wax finish.

Again, remember that right now we are only trying to determine what finish we have, later we will decide how to restore and care for the floor.

SHELLACS/WATERTHANES

Over the years several experimental finishes were used. Some only lasted a year or two on the market, and water-based shellacs were one of these test seals. They were resinous type seals, but were rather soft. And very susceptible to water spotting, turning the surface white, but they did provide a medium seal, better than oils. The older water-based finishes, more a test product, were fazed out of the market rather quickly because they were not as good as the solvent base permanent finishes.

OTHER FINISHES

The only other finish that might confuse us is the acrylic impregnated floors (because it is not really a finish, but a specially treated wood). They have the appearance of an oil-sealed floor. These floors are best detected by chipping away a tiny bit of the surface or finding an end view. Look for stain all the way through the wood. This is a good indication that it is acrylic flooring. These floors are found mostly in retail stores, malls, and high traffic areas. The wood is treated in a large vacuum chamber—all the air is sucked out of the chamber, then the color (stain) and acrylic seal mixture is injected into this chamber. The color and acrylic fills the microscopic voids in the wood, treating the wood throughout.

Wood Condition

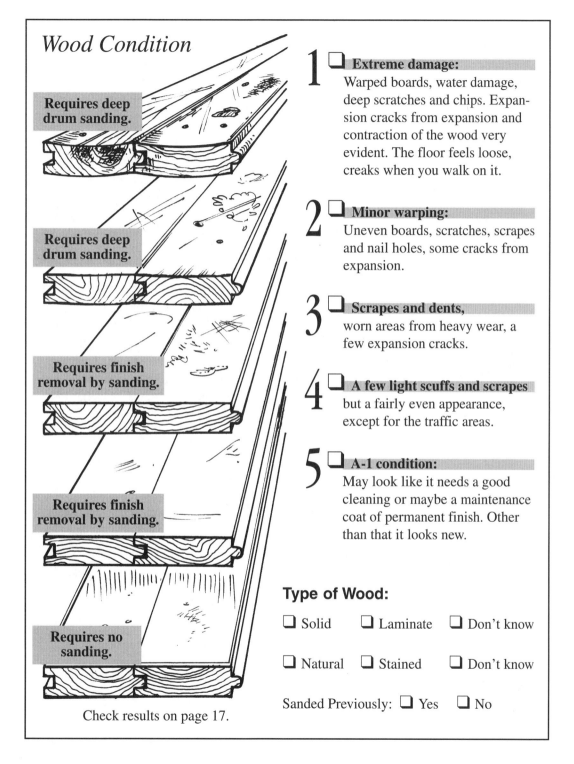

Requires deep drum sanding.

Requires deep drum sanding.

Requires finish removal by sanding.

Requires finish removal by sanding.

Requires no sanding.

Check results on page 17.

1 ☐ **Extreme damage:**
Warped boards, water damage, deep scratches and chips. Expansion cracks from expansion and contraction of the wood very evident. The floor feels loose, creaks when you walk on it.

2 ☐ **Minor warping:**
Uneven boards, scratches, scrapes and nail holes, some cracks from expansion.

3 ☐ **Scrapes and dents,**
worn areas from heavy wear, a few expansion cracks.

4 ☐ **A few light scuffs and scrapes**
but a fairly even appearance, except for the traffic areas.

5 ☐ **A-1 condition:**
May look like it needs a good cleaning or maybe a maintenance coat of permanent finish. Other than that it looks new.

Type of Wood:

☐ Solid   ☐ Laminate   ☐ Don't know

☐ Natural   ☐ Stained   ☐ Don't know

Sanded Previously: ☐ Yes   ☐ No

15

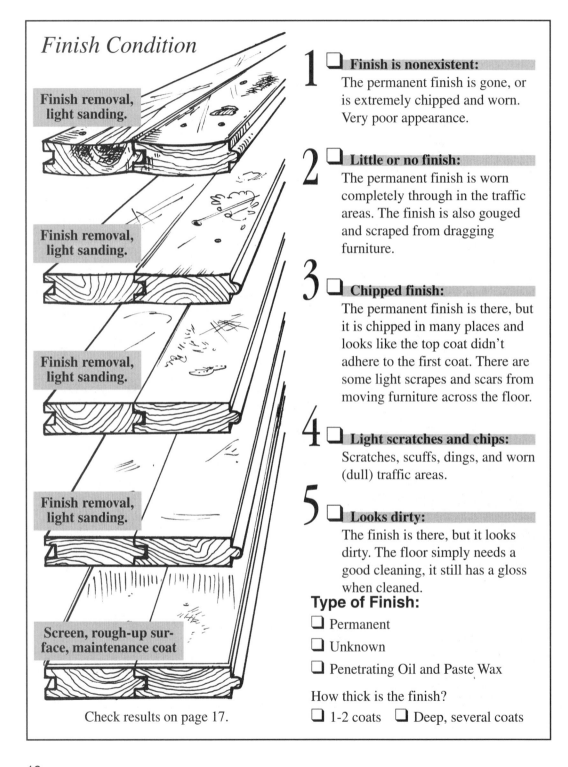

Finish Condition

Finish removal, light sanding.

Finish removal, light sanding.

Finish removal, light sanding.

Finish removal, light sanding.

Screen, rough-up surface, maintenance coat

Check results on page 17.

1 ❑ **Finish is nonexistent:**
The permanent finish is gone, or is extremely chipped and worn. Very poor appearance.

2 ❑ **Little or no finish:**
The permanent finish is worn completely through in the traffic areas. The finish is also gouged and scraped from dragging furniture.

3 ❑ **Chipped finish:**
The permanent finish is there, but it is chipped in many places and looks like the top coat didn't adhere to the first coat. There are some light scrapes and scars from moving furniture across the floor.

4 ❑ **Light scratches and chips:**
Scratches, scuffs, dings, and worn (dull) traffic areas.

5 ❑ **Looks dirty:**
The finish is there, but it looks dirty. The floor simply needs a good cleaning, it still has a gloss when cleaned.

Type of Finish:
❑ Permanent
❑ Unknown
❑ Penetrating Oil and Paste Wax

How thick is the finish?
❑ 1-2 coats   ❑ Deep, several coats

Wood Condition Chart Results

(See page 15.)

If your floor is a "1" or a "2," it needs to be flattened or leveled. This requires a deep or complete sanding with a drum sander—a job for the professionals. If you go after it with a buffer, you will smooth the surface, but it will not give you the "flat" that you need. It will just "round" the high spots.

A "3" and "4" require finish removal and light sanding which can be achieved with a buffer or square buff.

If your floor is a "5," usually a maintenance coat of permanent finish will be sufficient.

Finish Condition Chart Results

(See page 16.)

A "1," "2," or "3" here requires finish removal and light sanding (if it's not a 1 or 2 on *Wood Condition*). For "4" and "5" use a screen to rough up the surface and apply a maintenance coat of permanent finish.

If these tests don't give you any more insight into what you are dealing with, don't worry. Even a mystery floor can be dealt with, and at least we know what we aren't dealing with!

If you run into a weird finish or combination finish, the remedy is almost always to sand and refinish.

Chapter Two

New WOOD Floors?
The Choice Is YOURS!

Choosing a New Wood Floor and How to Choose Wisely

In most communities there are dozens of places to buy wood floors, plus many installers and specialized contractors. Not only are there dozens of places to buy, but once there, you have to choose from hundreds of styles, types, sizes, colors, and blends. It's wonderful, but overwhelming!

We have an incredible choice of material, quality, style, and features. It gets confusing because you'll find planks, strips, parquet, flats, walnut, maple, teak, fir, hardwood, oak, hickory, koa, even exotic species. Dealers and installers also have a menu of finishes that would mystify the League of Nations—Swedish, Danish, Germanish, Western, Eastern, laminated, natural, weathered, bleached, stained, etc., etc.

Wood flooring will last a lifetime and it is nice to have all of these choices. If you make a good choice you will be happy, and your investment will pay off!

The manufacturer's role in all this is to take raw material and make it into usable wood flooring—and they're doing a great job! We have some of the best products ever today. Yet, I was surprised when I talked to some manufacturers recently at a wood floor convention. They washed their hands of any other part of the process, and had no advice at all to offer on the type of finish to use or maintenance procedures. They gladly passed that on to the dealer or installer. Manufacturers spend a lot to educate their dealers about wood, its limits and strong points—so listen up!

I have faith in local dealers and installers. Although they aren't the maintenance experts and seldom have good cleaning advice, they are the best for helping to choose the best wood possible for a particular location. They know the best wood for your climate and intended use, whether it be in the kitchen, living room, or bedroom.

HERE IS WHAT I RECOMMEND

1 Visit different dealers in your area and ask for their wood floor expert. If they say "He/She isn't here, may I help you?" Leave and go back when the most knowledgeable wood floor person is there. Tell the "expert" what your floor goal is, i.e., kitchen, entry, dining, living room, den, etc., and what kind of use the area will receive and any specific conditions it will have to endure. Ask questions and look around, listen for personal experiences like "I have this is my home" or "We installed ten of those last year." If all their advice is hearsay, take it in but don't take it to the bank.

Be aware if you go to a carpet/tile store, they will push pre-finished wood, or even the laminate fake woods. Visit at least one company whose only business is wood floors, so that you will have their expertise.

2 Visit or call the installer or wood contractors. Some may not have a fancy showroom, or none at all, but are often more qualified then a retail outlet to give information based on practical experience.

> **WARNING—Some of the so-called "experts" can say some pretty ridiculous things. That is why I recommend visiting many dealers. After a while you will be able to weed out the new salespeople and find the most reputable dealers or contractors in your area.**

3 Visit and view the flooring installed, if possible. If you can, look at floors and finishes that have been in for a year or two. Nothing beats seeing it in the "flesh" and people with wood floors love to show them off—WOW! They will welcome you!

The manufacturer and dealer want more than anything for you to be happy with your floor—so take your time until you feel good about it. Go to the "Parade of Homes." This is when contractors set up several new homes to show off their handiwork, and they allow the public to go through them for a week or two. A display of this type may have a different name in your area. But go, and take the business cards of the wood floor installers and contractors there, take note of the

colors, designs, and finishes you like and dislike. Talk to the contractor on the home with the floor you admire—he might have installed it himself. Most contractors will subcontract a job like this out (that means have the job done by a full-time wood floor contractor). Find out who installed the floors, and call and talk to them.

4 Pick the style, colors, and price you want and then sleep on it before making the final decisions. Avoid weird colors and trendy designs. Remem-

ber, this is a permanent installation, part of your home, not a carpet that can be changed often. A wood floor will last centuries and still be attractive and in style if you make the right decisions.

Here are some considerations

Cost

Cost is the number one consideration, to most people, when they look at a wood floor purchase. Our tendency is to want save a bunch of money up front, but with wood floors as with most purchases, you will reap the rewards of quality fifteen or twenty years down the road.

You can buy parquet and other pre-finished squares and strips at retail tile flooring outlets, or even home hardware stores, right beside the stick-down tile, for around two dollars per square foot. These may seem really inexpensive, but after considering the cost of adhesives and labor, a hidden cost, you might be spending almost as much as on a professionally installed floor. There are engineered and pre-finished floors that run up to five to six dollars per square foot. These are better than the cheapie grades, and are fine for low-traffic areas. The top quality, pre-finished products often cost the same or sometimes more than a 3/4" solid hardwood floor, eight to ten dollars per

square foot installed. Of course these figures are only general guidelines. With wood prices going up these figures will change, but it gives you a general idea of the cost of the different options.

The best deal, in my opinion, is solid wood. It runs seven to nine dollars per square foot installed and finished. One local wood floor company said they could install a solid 3/4" oak number two common (meaning the wood has some strange grain and slight color difference) for around seven to eight dollars per square foot installed and finished. This would be as durable as the premium, but not as perfect and uniform in appearance—some people actually prefer it because it has "more personality."

Type of Wood

The most readily available woods for flooring are oak, maple, and walnut. Any other wood such as Honduran Mahogany and Brazilian woods, or some of the more famous exotic woods, will most likely be a special order. And often the cost is prohibitive to the average homeowner.

I would choose the oak or maple, good hardwood, whichever the dealer recommends as best for your area. Use the dealer's or installer's expertise, but don't let them make the decision for you. If you spent two years in the Peace Corps and want a piece of that country, choose Brazilian Mahogany! Remember, the finish will be the most important factor in the ease of maintenance.

Pine and softer woods are available, but because of the small demand for these woods in flooring they are costly also and need to be special ordered. The softer woods have a place, but aren't as durable and feasible in high-traffic areas, such as kitchens or a commercial building.

I saw an interesting thing in a trade magazine, some companies are salvaging old beams from hundred-year-old buildings to recut them and use them for pine flooring. Another company in the South is using scuba gear and retrieving old growth pine logs that have been forgotten after they sunk over one hundred years ago. They have been preserved underwater by the pitch all that time and still make excellent furniture and wood floors.

Finish

Finish is the number one consideration. **I can't stress the importance of a good finish enough!** Every time I give wood floor advice, input on a decision to refinish, etc., it always depends on the integrity of the finish. The right choice here can make or break your wood floor experience.

A pre-finished floor is one option to choose from when considering installing a wood floor. Most have an ultraviolet-cured polyurethane that make a tough wear layer. The finish is applied under controlled circumstances and several coats are applied. The cheaper pre-finished floors often have only one or two skimpy coats. The more expensive floors have seven to ten cured coats of polyurethane.

I prefer a floor finished on-site because it fills the cracks and seams better. Many installers make it a practice of putting one more coat of finish on a pre-finished floor immediately after installation, or after a year of use. This gives the floor added overall protection in the seams and cracks.

The bottom line is, there are at least twenty finish options, and this is the most important decision you will make on your wood floor. This is where I feel many dealers fall short. They recommend a pre-finished floor, but don't give you the pros and cons of that floor. The dealers often make it sound like no maintenance is needed after you install the floor. Read Chapter Five about finish pros and cons BEFORE you decide, it gives a good comparison of finishes.

Durability

Solid oak or other hard wood is the best choice. The harder the wood the more durable it will be at resisting dents. The wear will be on the finish. Notice I didn't say hardwood. The term "hardwood" is given to certain classes of trees and may have no relation to the hardness of the wood. Oaks and maples tend to be the most durable for a floor, but different areas of the country feature different wood. Ask the local dealer or installer what they feel is the toughest wood for

your particular area.

Some of the softer woods give us a unique appearance but are less durable. Some people prefer the soft wood called pine—it is less durable, but has its own beauty.

A properly installed, pre-finished wood floor is almost as durable as hardwood but is limited in refinishing and repair options.

I am impressed with the durability of the acrylic impregnated floors also. Acrylic impregnation is done on both solid wood and engineered floors. This finish is designed for a more commercial use such as in retail stores, malls, bars,

dance floors, etc., and is not meant to be refinished or to have high gloss. They require their own special maintenance system which usually includes spraying and buffing.

No wood floor is going to wear like a ceramic tile floor. More care and maintenance is required with wood. However, wood lasts, looks good, and stays in style longer than other floor coverings.

Advantages of Wood

Over the long haul, ease of maintenance might be the most important consideration in buying a wood floor. Maintenance requirements vary with the finish on a wood floor. No matter what floor you choose, if it is not sealed well (back to the importance of the finish) maintenance will be a nightmare! Best results are obtained from an installed floor with three coats of good finish or a top quality pre-finished floor. The maintenance process is explained in Chapter Seven. When making your new floor decision make sure you match the right finish to the use your floor will get. See pages 58-61.

Wood acts as a great camouflager, it looks great most of the time even though it may be filthy. I know people who were told to never mop their wood floor, and they haven't deep cleaned it for years. This is hard for me to imagine, because I clean and mop my wood floor at least once a week. Wood may hide our cleaning sins, disguise some day-to-day neglect, but it is not good practice to let dirt build up because the dirt will eventually damage the finish.

Do-It-Yourself?

Can you really do the whole job from installing, to sanding, to finishing yourself? Anything is possible! If you are handy with tools and familiar with building I might suggest giving it a try.

I have done several things myself that I probably had no business doing. Once I decided to paint my car. To make a long story short and a quick point, I did it and a pretty darn good job, too. I learned a lot about paints and doing things over. I learned that even the smallest imperfections will show up—things I was sure the paint would hide—after you get a vehicle painted. But I didn't save much money doing it myself and I didn't get a premium job. I did, however, learn that I didn't want to paint cars for a living. Overall it was a rewarding, educational experience.

So if you are like me and enjoy the satisfaction of doing and learning, give it a shot. If the only reason you want to install the floor yourself is to save tons of money, be careful. Often before you are through you will end up spending more and getting a less than professional job. Contractors and wood floor installers take the risk. If something isn't right (if it is their fault) they will fix it for nothing. If we do it ourselves we are stuck with it.

If you choose to install a solid wood floor, be prepared and do some research! Pick up some installation and sanding videos—watch and take notes. This book wasn't designed to teach those trade secrets.

Chapter Three

Outwitting Wood's Worst Enemies—PREVENTION

How to Make Your Wood Floor Last Practically Forever!

What wounds wood. Let's protect what we have!

Before we start caring for, fixing, and finishing our wood floors, we need to STOP the reasons they need extra care and fixing and finishing (and refinishing) in the first place. I've seen wood floors in old homes that are still great today. I've also seen wood floors that need replaced after only a couple of years of use. It is surprising how many wood floor owners know only one taboo: WATER.

At a recent wood floor convention, I met several contractors with different approaches to YOU the customer. I talked to two guys who told me horror stories of when they first started. They said they went in, finished the floor, and got out, leaving not a business card or any other trace of their existence. When the cus-

tomer would accidentally happen to catch them on the job and ask about the finish, "What was the best way to keep the floor looking good?" The contractor would come back with, "No agua, no comprendo, I only the worker." He was the head boss!

That was twenty plus years ago, and I found it hard to believe they were still in business with their attitudes. Now don't get me wrong, he did an impeccable job, but the customer was left without a clue as to what to do now. Maybe the customer isn't upset at first, but a year later when they need maintenance help and can't find the installer then they will get hot under the collar and call me.

My conversation with an up-and-coming floor man on the way to the airport gave me hope for the industry. He explained that he personally sat down with the new owners and explained the "do's and don'ts." He had a form and he would have the customer check off the boxes as he explained each item, and then he left his business card, mobile phone number, and the works with them. In six months the boss would call the owner and ask them if they had any questions and would offer a free inspection to catch any problem areas, like excessive wear areas, etc. Guess which company is so busy they can't handle all of the business!

10 Truths About Wood Floors

This is more information on wood floors than most contractors even know, let alone pass on to their customers.

✔ 1. True Grit, Sand & Soil

It isn't by accident that this is first! Sand, grit, and foreign matter are the number one enemy of wood floors. Things like toys, steel filings, chips of plastics, hard food crumbs, nutshells, and all sorts of tiny morsels of mud, dirt, and gravel will get on your nice floor from both outside and inside sources. Combined with walking, running, sliding, dragging things across the floor, etc., it becomes perfect sandpaper to grind, dull, and scratch and dent the surface and finish. This is the biggest enemy of all flooring—tile and carpet, as well as wood. **PREVENTION IS A MUST!**

It is not always a crime to get dirt on the floor, it will happen—the crime is not getting it off. Get into the habit of sweeping, dust mopping, or vacuuming daily. It only takes a minute if you have the right tools (see Chapter Seven).

Good matting is the best way to keep this damaging grit off your wood floor. Don't underestimate the value of good commercial door mats or "walkoff" mats.

On the outside of the entry, I recommend a tough, aggressive AstroTurf® mat. This will get the heavier soil, mud, grass, etc. Inside the entry use a nylon or olefin mat. They are softer and designed to capture dust and dirt and dry your shoes as you enter.

Consider 3'x 4' size mats. This is big enough to catch at least a couple of steps, and a bunch of dirt. These can be purchased from a janitorial supply store or from the Cleaning Center (see page 77).

✓2. Water

Almost everyone with wood floors is terrified by the thought of water on wood. It is true that prolonged contact with water and air will eventually warp a poorly finished wood floor. Prolonged contact with water will swell the grain of wood and cause the finish to chip off. Water can be very damaging to wood, if used improperly, but remember too that wooden ships last hundreds of years. The degree to which you can use water depends on the integrity of the finish. Wood floors, if finished properly, can be mopped and cleaned with cleaning solutions and water. In fact, often the only

way to clean them well is with a water-base cleaner. Wood like anything else, gets dirty, and how can we clean it? We have to wash it.

Water can't get to wood if it has a good finish. On a well-finished floor dampness never touches the wood because we're cleaning the finish, not the wood itself. On porous or poorly finished wood, avoid water or else use it quickly. On a well-sealed floor you could build a swimming pool.

✓3. High Heels

High heels are trouble on the hoof for most wood. Millions of beautiful wood floors are "dimpled" with those tiny spikes, which are permanent damage. It seems impossible that a 105-pound woman armed with a pair of fashion footwear can exert as much force as an automobile or an elephant. Tests show that the pressure at the point of contact is as much as 2,000 pounds—that is from a common ordinary high heel in good repair. If one is worn or damaged (so the nail is exposed) it can exceed a force of 8,000 psi (which can even crush hardened

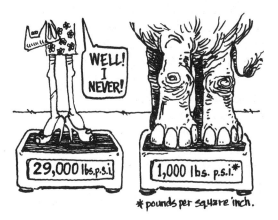

WELL! I NEVER!

29,000 lbs. p.s.i.   1,000 lbs. p.s.i.*

*pounds per square inch.

concrete). Some people ask guests to take their shoes off before walking into their homes. It's not a bad idea, I'm not there yet, although I do watch for and de-shoe the high heelers. Needless to say, cleats or hard-soled boots, etc., should not be allowed on the floor either, so watch for family or friends running though the house with softball or soccer cleats.

This is a tough one. I don't know how fanatical you want to be, so make family and friends aware of your floor and decide about guests.

✓ 4. Furniture

Furniture can sit in one place for ten years and not do any harm, but that one time you drag a couch or entertainment center across the floor can cause more permanent and severe damage than a year or two of foot traffic. Not long ago, a young couple came into my store and said the movers had dragged a piano across their new floor and caused a fairly deep scrape. They were in looking for a quick fix—sorry, there is none! Most often the floor would have to be refinished to solve a damage problem like this.

Get plenty of friends with good backs when moving. Always lift when moving or use a dolly. Avoid dragging furniture like the plague. If lifting is out of the question, be sure and get a dolly or something with wheels—big soft wheels, not metal wheels

Keep furniture legs in good repair. A loose or wobbly leg can dig into the finish of the floor every time you sit down and get up.

Rocking chairs look good on a wood floor, but try to keep an area rug under them, or buy the glider type rockers that don't have runners.

Use felt pads on contact areas when possible. This provides some cushioning and won't scratch. Avoid the Teflon coasters, they might slide across the floor easily, but can trap sand and grit in the surface and act like sandpaper. Vacuum off the felt or carpet-like surface protectors regularly, they too will collect dirt and eventually act like sandpaper if left dirty.

✓ 5. Dropping Dings

Dropping things can cause severe damage to a wood floor. Any object weighing a couple of pounds or even ounces that falls to the floor will dent it. And sharp objects can cut it. Accidents will happen. My kids are famous for carrying things bigger than they are… give them a hand. Don't let them practice juggling on the wood floor, either. A little care to keep potentially droppable items out of the wood floor area is smart and easy. Watch out for chairs that fall over easily, dishes, heavy cleaning gear, toys, decorative metal objects, sports equipment like barbells, weights, etc. No need for a big alarm—just a little thinking ahead keeps wood floors happier. So use some common sense here.

✔ 6. Spills

Spills will happen and a properly finished wood floor can take them, but don't let them stay. Spills that remain (especially pet accidents, food, cleaners, alcohol, oil, blood, etc.) can and will create a chemical reaction that can permanently damage the wood or its finish. Just wiping it up now will save the floor and save someone from falling, too, and that's a good deal for all concerned. In my kitchen I have a refrigerator that dispenses water and ice from the door, for instance. Often an ice cube or two will miss the cup and scoot across the wood floor. Be aware of potential problems like this and keep an eye open, especially if the kids aren't too diligent about picking up the ice cubes. Common sense says *cleaning it up QUICK makes good sense"!*

✔ 7. Sun

The sun is great for wood when it is still alive and growing, as it is for most living things. But once that wood is cut into board feet, direct sun rays can fade and discolor it, and this includes the wood in floors. Some older varnishes and other finishes will also yellow in the sun.

Wood floors that are in front of a window with too-often-open drapes and too many sunny days may bleach, darken, or even dry out. Remember also, the darker the wood, the more heat it attracts. Sunlight is okay, but use a sheer liner inside your drapes, it will direct the ultraviolet rays away, and just be aware of the potential damage.

✔ 8. Harsh Cleaners and Other Concoctions

I've had people confess to using all sorts of stuff on their wood floors, even though most installers and manufacturers go to the other extreme and tell us to use nothing. Maybe we pick something up from a hint and tip section, or try a friend's remedy. Or maybe we just experiment. Wood is rather self-sustaining, especially if finished correctly, and doesn't need special oils and waxes. One of the worst things we can use on wood floors is "vegetable oil soaps." They can

buildup and cause havoc when it is time to put a maintenance coat of permanent finish on the floor. The best cleaner for finished wood flooring is a neutral pH cleaner like Top Sheen or Wood Wash. These are designed to get tough soil without damaging or dulling the finish. (See Chapter Seven.) The best bet is DON'T EXPERIMENT and get rid of all those goofy remedies.

9. Buildup

Letting your wood floor go without proper cleaning will eventually cause buildup of dust, dirt, grease, wax, etc. Buildup makes a floor look bad and can cause yellowing of the finish. And before long it will mean a need to "strip" or deep clean your wood floor. This isn't fun for you or the floor, because it means lots of machines, cleaners, chemical strippers and water, plus the process of bringing the floor back to normal afterward is risky and costly. Good regular maintenance and keeping wax off non-traffic areas is your best defense against buildup. Find a maintenance program (See Chapter Seven) that works for you and your floor and stick with it!

10. Vacuums (with beater)

Beater bars or brushes on a vacuum are only great for carpets. Used on wood, the rotating bar or brushes can cause dents. The turning roller bar can also pick up a piece of grit and force it into the wood, chipping or scratching (wrecking) the finish. Be careful of thresholds between carpets and wood floors. The roller or bar really "beats" these up. Suction-only vacuums are great on wood, but make sure you aren't creating scratches by pulling and pushing the machine around the floor and that the vacuum isn't damaging the floor in other ways.

*Oops…
one more!*

11. Mats and Rugs

Mats are one of the most important preventative measures. Interior mats finish taking dust and dirt of the foot, plus absorb moisture. But they can also be a potential problem. Some mats and throw rugs have vinyl, plastic, or rubber backs that can trap and keep moisture under the mat on the floor for weeks. Wait until the floor is completely dry before putting the mat in place. Pick them up often and check for moisture. If this turns out to be a continuing problem, consider removing the mats. AstroTurf® mats outside your entrances help to stop dirt, mud, grass, sand, rocks, etc., and really save your floor—not to mention your time cleaning! Mats should be long enough for at least two strides.

And now some last little sneaky things to keep an eye out for...

- Drips and leaks from faucets and house plants, and rain through an open window if allowed to sit on your wood floor, can literally leave their mark.

- Steel wool is used a lot in refinishing wood. But don't use it to clean with, because although it feels soft it can scratch and cut especially if used dry. Even the tiny filings from steel wool can grind.

- Wicker baskets often placed around the pots of house plants, set right on the floor. Plant food, etc., collects unseen beneath them and can stain, darken, even rot the floor.

Here is a quick recap of the potential problems to refresh your memory:

- Grit, sand and soil
- Water
- High heels
- Furniture moving
- Dropping dings
- Spills
- Sun
- Harsh cleaners
- Buildup
- Vacuum beater bars or brushes
- Moisture under mats and rugs

"Every contractor should sit down and review with the customer these potential problem areas. The customer will be happier and the floors will last and look better longer."

To Do:

☐ Mat all entrances.

☐ Sweep or vacuum often—damp mop when needed
(see Chapter Seven).

☐ Prevent surprise water sources (overflowing dishwasher,
open windows, overflow from plants).

☐ Head off damaging footwear.

☐ When moving furniture, get extra bodies and lift, don't drag.

☐ No juggling on wood floors.

☐ Clean up spills immediately when they happen.

☐ Use proper cleaning equipment.

☐ Do frequent visual inspections for future problems.

☐ Schedule an inspection after six months.

*I have reviewed with contractor and understand these prevention
methods and potential damage problems.*

_____   _____
Homeowner signature   Contractor signature

Chapter Four

Preparing a Floor for Refinishing: Sanding & Stripping

There are times and places when sanding and stripping a floor and then refinishing it is the only way, but remember that we are approaching this ambitious process from a totally different perspective than that of the professional refinisher/installer. The professional is looking at the floor with all his equipment, expertise, and help. There is only one option in his eyes and that is to use his big equipment to sand the floor into readiness for refinishing.

We, on the other hand, are looking at it with our limited expertise, cost constraints, etc. When we go out and talk to a professional about the process he wonders why anyone would think of doing it any other way. Some of these guys will even make you think you are stupid or crazy. They don't intend to put you down, they just think there is a better way, and if you

owned the equipment they do and had sanded the hundreds of floors they have, there wouldn't be another option for you either.

This chapter is designed to present the easiest, safest, and most effective way of preparing a wood floor for refinishing, other than having a professional do it for you.

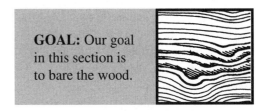

GOAL: Our goal in this section is to bare the wood.

It seems scary when we start talking about sanding and stripping, but it's not as bad as you imagine. Now that we know the condition of our floor, and the results we want to achieve when we are finished.

HOW TO DO IT YOURSELF

Removing the Finish

For removal of a heavy buildup of permanent finish we have two choices, sanding or chemical removal. If there is a thick coat or several coats of finish on there (years of buildup), I recommend using a chemical remover before sanding. If the buildup is light to moderate, sanding will be quick and efficient. A commercial machine will cut through even the biggest buildup.

Chemical Paint and Varnish Removers

If you find the finish is built up because of years of recoating with varnish or urethanes, it can be sanded off, but will take a lot of time and waste a bunch of sandpaper. On most floors that have been treated with coat after coat of varnish, the wood itself is in great shape because the heavy layer of varnish or finish protected the wood. For this reason deep (drum) sanding is not always necessary, even though it would effectively remove the finish. For removal of buildup the easier and faster method is using a paint and varnish remover. We often call it paint stripper, but don't confuse it with wax

stripper. Some contractors like to "burn" finish buildup off with a sander, but for us the removers work better and avoid the waste of all that costly sandpaper. The stripper removal process is a messy job, but much faster than trying to screen or sand it all off.

NOTE: arrange for plenty of ventilation before you start, because this stuff really stinks up the place. Wear rubber gloves and goggles, too, and follow ALL label precautions about open flames and sparks!

Find a compatible stripper. You can find strippers/paint removers at all paint stores and most home centers and hardware stores. They come in a variety of styles from thin to thick paste, light, medium and heavy-duty strength. I like the thicker stuff and I will pay the extra for heavy-duty remover, it will usually do the job in one application. Some will work better than others. Get a sample or a small container of the one you have in mind to use and following the directions on the label, test in a closet or under furniture.

Once you find the product for the job, brush it on liberally (don't skimp). I've found it is better to use a little more up front than have to reapply it a second time. After a few minutes it will start to bubble up and look like wrinkled skin. Don't get in a hurry to remove it now, as there might still be spots that aren't releasing (bubbling up).

Don't spread the stripper over the entire floor at one time. Work in manageable areas. Strippers have to be wet to work, as soon as they dry out they stop working. In some areas the finish will absorb the stripper and dry up. All it takes is a little bit more stripper in that area, and WHAMMO! It will release!

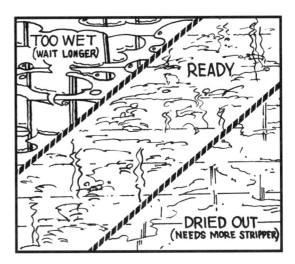

CAUTION: Be careful not to splash stripper on baseboards, walls, doors, and furniture, or any painted surface, even the refrigerator—it will remove the paint!

Be ready for a big mess. This stuff has softened or "re-emulsified" the finish and now it has to be scraped up with a putty knife or a large sheetrock blade and disposed of. Get a couple of plastic five-gallon buckets and scoop up the finish into them.

You might find some stubborn spots where the old finish is still adhering and you might have to reapply stripper in those spots. This problem is common around the edges of the floor and under furniture, where the finish didn't get much traffic or wear.

I've also seen floors that need two complete applications. Most strippers are good for two or three coats of finish. If a floor has been recoated several times, the stripper might only go a couple of coats deep then stop. If you have a really bad buildup, remove the first pile of gunk and apply a fresh coat of stripper, it will attack the bottom coats and take the rest of the finish off. Don't be concerned if it doesn't look perfect, a few stubborn spots can be sanded off easily.

After the old finish is removed your floor is ready for the sanding process, we are down to that bare wood!

NOTE: Some states are very particular about the disposal of this waste. Some classify it as hazardous. Check with your local area for proper disposal procedures. Most areas will have a hazardous drop-off point free of charge for households. Each county and state is different, however, so check it out.

WAX REMOVAL
Stripping off the Old Wax!

Wax stripping may be done before simply rewaxing or to prepare the floor for sanding or refinishing. Always remove any wax before sanding or screening, even if it is only one coat. The wax will clog the sanding screen or paper and make the job miserable!

Water-Based Wax Removers: Are They a No-No?

Many contractors will tell you the only way to get wax off safely is with deep sanding, so they tell you to never wax. They say water-based strippers are not safe to use on wood floors. I quizzed contractors about stripping wax off a wood floor and they said sure it can be done, and they do it occasionally, but their crews are used to sanding. If they stop and change everything to strip wax off, it would cause more confusion than it is worth to them, so they

often choose to just use up more sandpaper. It costs them something, but it also saves them the time and money of switching gears.

The idea of waxing alarms most wood floor people because of the damage that can occur from using too much water. If you need to remove wax, you can do the following.

Follow the stripping instructions here to have great results, but FOLLOW THE DIRECTIONS! Work in small areas and be sure and use a wet/dry vacuum. A wet/dry vacuum is a MUST for this job. A buffer, in my opinion, is also a necessity. These two tools will speed the process up and eliminate any possible floor damage.

If you have to strip wax off a large area get a buffer. These are the machines you see the janitor scrubbing and polishing floors with in schools and stores. A buffer can be rented at a rental shop for a few dollars a day. Look for a 16"-17", they are the easiest to handle and you can use it for both scrubbing and sanding. Be sure and try it out in the rental shop so they can show you how it works. Buffers are tricky if you have never run one before. You can also use a long-handled hand scrubber like a Scrubbee Doo (see page 78). This is my pick for household scrubbing, but on wood, speed is of the essence, so I recommend a large buffer.

Start with a good heavy-duty wax stripper. Wax strippers are found at janitorial supply stores or available from the Cleaning Center (see "Mop Stripper" page 80). The kind you buy in the supermarket are often slow and ineffective on

40

wax buildup. Spread the stripper on an area, about 10'x10', and scrub with a black or brown scrubbing pad. Go over it once, wait two minutes, and go back over it in the other direction.

If you use a heavy-duty stripper and a buffer, this will remove the wax in a hurry. Follow closely behind with the wet/dry vacuum and pick up the dissolved solution. Be sure not to leave small puddles and spills. It's a good idea to have some help with this process, and an extra person makes it go much better. Go to the next 10'x10' section of the floor and continue the same way until the wax is removed from the entire floor.

After removing the wax, rinse the entire floor with a neutralizing solution. Mix one cup of vinegar to a gallon of water.

Now the floor is ready to sand or apply acrylic polish (wax). Water won't hurt the floor unless it is left on there to sit for a long period of time. This will contradict many wood people's advice. Their pat answer is *never, never, never use water on wood.* I've used water on wood floors hundreds of times and had great results, but I've also warped a couple of floors from leaving it on too long.

Water coming in contact with bare wood can raise the grain a bit, but it will not damage the wood if removed quickly and the raised grain will be smoothed out by sanding. It's contact with water, such as sitting water, that can cause warped boards and cracks to appear. Much water damage to wood floors happens from water seeping around and under poorly finished floors and getting to the unfinished underside of the wood. A flooded or damp basement or crawl space can also damage a floor from the bottom up. This has nothing to do with the cleaning process, but it's the cleaning process that often gets blamed.

Now we proceed to sanding.

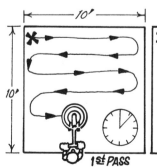

1ˢᵗ PASS   2ⁿᵈ PASS

Sanding

Sanding is another way of getting the finish off the surface and getting down to the bare wood. Sanding also helps to even out the wood and remove any stains or scratches. We almost always think of a big sanding machine when we think of sanding out wood floors. But we are going to use a commercial buffer with a sanding screen or disk.

For home use we have two options, the rotary buffer seen in every school, church, and large business building. Also very effective and easy to use are the oscillating scrubbers—such as the square buff. They work like an orbiting hand sander but are much larger and heavier. The sanding surface is about 10"x24". Oscillating scrubbers can be found at some rental shops and specialty stores that carry wood floor do-it-yourself products.

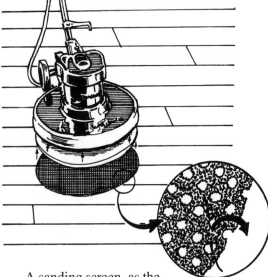

A sanding screen, as the name implies, is much like a screen on a screen door, but is made out of abrasive material. Like sandpaper, the sanding screen comes in different grits (coarseness). Screens are made to fit under a regular rotating round buffer pad. The advantage of the open-mesh construction of a screen is that the particles sanded off will pass through it, so a screen won't clog up like plain sandpapers do. You can also use sandpaper disks. These are simply sandpaper cut into a circle to fit the buffer.

Sanding screens will work on most any surface, but on occasion wax will plug up even a screen. To help in this situation you can use a heavier grade of screen. I just found a company that supplies sanding screens in a 16/36 grit. These grits are usually found only in the paper sanding disks. Using a coarser grit will require more sanding afterward with finer screens to remove the deeper scratches from the coarser paper.

Sanding Screen or Sandpaper Disk?

The choice depends on the job at hand. Overall I feel screens are easier to use and give more even results, especially on final preparation. It's what the professionals use after they sand with their large machines. Disks are sometimes more handy when the finish is heavy and you didn't use a stripper on it, because disks can cut through some finishes faster than screens and this saves some time. If you plan to sand off a heavy coat of finish or layer of wax, plan on starting with a coarse disk and finishing with finer screens. Some rental places only have one or the other, so look in several places.

Grits

The screens or disks used for sanding floors are rated similar to sandpaper. The lower the number, the coarser it is. For example: 36-60 grit cuts into the wood faster and will remove deep scratches or stains but will leave deeper sanding marks. A medium coarseness, 80-100, will not cut through the finish as fast, but will leave less sanding marks. A 120-150 grit is a finish grit that will smooth out the surface nicely. It is usually used to sand out the marks from the coarser paper.

The industry standard for sanding grits is three steps: first, 50 grit, then 80 grit, and finish with 100 grit. When using a sanding screen you can get away with two steps for most floors, start with 80 grit and then finish with 100 grit.

What is Needed

- A 16"-17" commercial buffer or square buff orbiting sander. These can be rented for $15 to $25 a day at a rental shop. They come with a drive block, which is what holds the scrubbing pad on. Buy one black or brown scrubbing pad. This will grip to the drive block and your screen then will grip to it. The screen can't connect directly to the drive block, it needs the pad.

- A good, sharp paint scraper to get seal and finish off corners, under radiators, etc.

- A hand oscillating sander for sanding edges and corners.

- A wet/dry vacuum. This helps with the dust control. It not only keeps the old finish from clogging up your sanding equipment or getting ground back into the floor as you sand , it also helps remove all the dust when you get ready to seal and finish.

- Dust masks for everyone working!

Plastic drop cloths to place over areas that you don't want dusty. Hang them over bookcases, doorways, etc.

That's it for now. Before get everything off the floor. It is impossible to work around objects.

Ready?

Put the drive pad on the buffer, then the buffing pad, and center the sanding screen on it. If possible start with an 80 grit screen, it will start sanding and cut the finish fast enough for most jobs. Some jobs require a coarser grit, 60 or even 36, but only use these in bad areas that need it, like uneven boards or areas with deep scratches and use the 80 grit in all the other areas. Remember if you use a coarser grit you will have to sand out deeper scratches with finer sanding screens.

Start the process by going over a large area. This will cut into the top surface layer, which tends to clog and dull the screen disk the fastest. You will use more screens at first, then as you get to the wood they will last longer. When a screen dulls turn it over and keep going. You will notice that a new screen will sand or cut faster. You can usually tell when sandpaper gets dull—it will glide over the floor and doesn't seem like it is removing anything. A dull screen will look about the same as a new screen, but it is worthless. Grab a new screen and keep going! I like to cover larger areas rather than work on small areas. This extends the life of the screen and speeds up the job and give you a more uniform job.

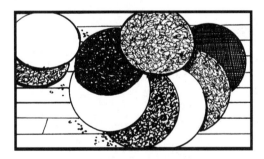

You will notice the edges are more stubborn than the center of the floor, this is because the edges usually have more buildup. After three or four times over an area, instead of the dust from the finish you will start getting wood dust. This means you are through the finish. Don't stop here, you will want to sand the wood down a little, depending on the scratches, dents, and discolorations in the floor.

You can remove 95%, if not all, of the imperfections with this method. If there is a spot or two that is deep and only can be removed by deep sanding, I would leave it, it is not worth deep sanding the entire floor for a couple of bad spots. After the new finish is applied these dents and scratches will hardly be noticeable.

Edges

You can get rather close to the edges with your buffer, and a square buff will get within inches, but in any case you will also need a small sander to get in close to the walls and corners. I use a Mikita palm orbital vibrating sander, it works great! It is important that you take care in sanding the edges to match the depth and texture of the sanding screen. If you do a great sanding job on the floor and give up on the edges you will have a picture frame effect, with the outside edges darker or lighter depending on whether you got not enough or too much of the finish is sanded off. You can also use a wood scraper here to get the bulk of the finish off before sanding.

Keep sanding the edges until the floor and edges are uniform. It takes a good eye to make sure you are ready to go on. Look at the floor, are there dirty areas that need more attention, like the traffic areas, usually in front of the couch or an entryway area? A trick that helps out here is to take a cleaning cloth and dampen it with mineral spirits or paint thinner (from a paint or home improvement store), and

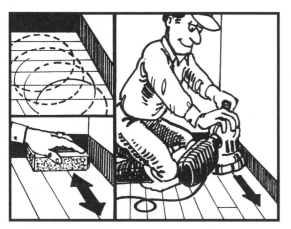

wipe a small area. This will give you a good idea of what the floor will look like when finished. Do this especially in problem areas. The mineral spirits will quickly evaporate off and you can continue to sand, if necessary, until you are satisfied.

> **NOTE: Most scratches and scars will not show up while sanding, but will stick out like a sore thumb when new finish is applied, so the mineral spirits will help you catch these bad spots.**

Even though this is the best way for an amateur to know how they are doing, some floor finishes specify not to use thinner or mineral spirits with them so read the label. Mineral spirits is more refined than paint thinner and will leave less residue.

READ ALL LABELS ON SEAL AND FINISH BEFORE YOU START THE FLOOR PREPARATION PROCESS!

Keep screening until you are satisfied. Unlike the drum sander, when screening you are not removing tons of wood, so you can take your time and make sure you have it right. This is where your good eye comes into play. Inspect the floor well before going on. Many times twenty more minutes spent checking and rescreening problem areas can make or break the entire job.

> **NOTE: The great thing about using a rotating buffer or orbiting square buff (over a drum sander) is that it is almost impossible to damage or ruin a wood floor with one. Sure it might take a bit longer to achieve your desired results, but the ease and safety benefits are worth it. The most damage I've seen from these machines is an amateur running a rotating buffer into the wall.**

Drum Sanding
Should I or Shouldn't I??

I'm a real do-it-yourselfer type of person. I like the adventure of most projects around the house. There are only a few projects I haven't tried. I have sanded quite a few floors, however, and if I were in your shoes, drum sanding is one of those things I would get a professional to do. You can do more damage in a couple of passes with a drum sander than by stampeding a herd of elephants over your floor.

One problem the do-it-yourselfer has is that we can't get the same equipment the pros use. A wood floor contractor told

me that even his best man would have trouble using the drum sander machines that are available for rent, typically old and out of adjustment.

If you are at all hesitant and don't feel up to the challenge don't risk it! If you are still determined to use a drum sander for deep sanding, do some research and check out some reference material about drum sanding. There are some good videos and how-to books on the subject. And try renting from a wood floor installer, they have better equipment.

Minor Repairs

Now inspect the floor carefully and fill the cracks and nail holes with wood putty. A trick the pros use is mixing sanding dust with carpenter's glue. I've had more luck with the commercial wood floor patching products than with the sawdust mixture. If the entire floor has cracks you might need to use a special

crack filler made especially for this. Crack filler is a semiliquid you trowel on the entire floor and then screen the floor again. It is important to use crack filler if you need it because it will prevent further damage to the floor by keeping water out from between the boards. Do this between your second and third sanding. Be

sure to let the filler dry thoroughly before you continue sanding. If there are deep scars, etc., use crack filler or putty. If the patched spot is large and noticeable, you can draw in the grain with a fine-tip permanent marker.

NOTE: Filler and putty take stain and seal differently than wood itself. Make sure the filler you choose matches the finished color of the wood as closely as possible. If you are going to stain your floor, pick the color of filler to match the stain. If you are simply going to use the natural wood color, be aware that wood will darken a bit when a clear finish is applied. The wipe-down trick with mineral spirits will give you a good idea how it will look.

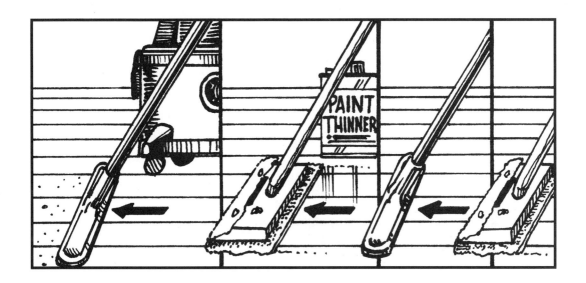

If there some big problems in isolated areas of your floor, a professional can cut these few boards out and replace them easily. If your floor has a few problems, it is probably well worth letting a professional help instead of experimenting on your own.

Final Preparation

After you are finished sanding, VACUUM THOROUGHLY and go over the whole floor with a painter's tack cloth (from a paint or home improvement store). Tack cloth is made of sticky—"tacky"—material that will pick up fine dust particles.

I use a terry cloth towel dampened with paint thinner to tack the entire floor. This gives you a good idea of how the floor will look when finished and picks up the dust at the same time. Wipe and vacuum any other surface in the area too that might have collected dust (door frames, window sills, etc.). Vacuum again and tack the floor with a tack cloth. I do this several times until I am confident all the dust is gone.

Now we are ready to apply the finish. Don't get to this step and wait a couple of days—be prepared to proceed with the finish shortly after sanding. This will prevent any new dust and dirt being brought in. If you delay, the moisture in the air will also cause the grain to raise and touch-up sanding and more cleaning and preparation will be required.

Contractors have their own special way of preparing a floor for finish. Some will rely on their vacuum alone to get the dust off the floor and never "tack" the floor until after the first seal coat. Some will tack with a cloth dampened with water. This will raise the grain slightly but usually not enough to notice. This requires another screening after the first coat of seal, then they tack the floor with a cloth barely dampened with water again.

Chapter Five

Time to FINISH What We Started!
This is where all your hard work pays off!

It is important to take care in the seal and finish process. In fact, it is crucial to achieve the desired results. Good news though, it isn't as difficult as you might think.

Most professionals break the finish process into two steps: seal and finish, and that is why they get paid big bucks. They know the key to getting a perfect floor, and it's simple.

Before Seal/Finish

Now is the time to stain, stencil, or bleach your floor—before sealing.

Always try this in a closet or an inconspicuous area first. This is something you may have to live with for the life of the wood so be sure of the desired look. Avoid trendy styles, wood floors will never go out of style (they never have), but colors, stencils, and stains can.

Even deep drum sanding won't remove some penetrating stains.

Dark, dark floors are harder to keep looking good. They will show the slightest dust or debris. Bleached or white-stained floors, on the other hand, will reflect light and any soil, dirt, scuff marks, etc., will stand out in high con-

trast. In some homes these may be the best colors for the style and decorations, but remember they will require more care.

I like a natural or slight stain. Remember, wood will darken to a slight amber when seal is applied. If in doubt test on a sample piece of flooring before you commit. Again, don't get carried away with anything outrageous.

First, let's discuss the difference between seal and finish. I mentioned these two terms several times earlier in the book, but it is important to really understand them. Ask any wood floor person, **"It ALL comes back to the FINISH!"** Not just the appearance of the floor, but the ease of maintenance to follow!

Seal

Seals are similar in chemical makeup to finishes, but are thinner in consistency, and contain less resins. Both seals and finishes have a percent of solids. This means that once they are dry (the solvents have evaporated out) X% of the product is still on the floor making up the finish. Have you ever left the lid off a paint or a finish can and then came back a week or month later to find a solid blob that is about a third of what you started with? That is the 30% solids after the 70% solvent has evaporated out.

Seals range from 8-12% solids while finishes are 30-40% solids. The important thing here is that we want the first coat to be less dense and more fluid so it can penetrate deep into the wood and seal it off from water and other forms of moisture. Penetration also allows the seal to adhere well to the wood so the finish won't peel or chip off. You will notice that when you put seal on it looks shiny but when it dries it is dull and appears to have disappeared. This is a good sign, and one good coat of seal is usually sufficient. If the floor was really "thirsty" a second coat of seal may be needed.

Finish, as I just said, is higher in solids and is designed as a top coat. If you simply apply finish to bare wood it has a tendency to sit on top and not penetrate or bond sufficiently (especially to poorly prepared wood) and will be prone to chip and peel off.

The best and hardest finishes are usually the ones with higher solids content. They will cost you a bit more, but are usually worth it!

FIRST apply one coat of seal. SECOND apply two to three coats of permanent finish. The following directions are the same for applying either.

How to Apply Seal/Finish

Seal/finish is one of the easiest of all coatings to apply. It is self-leveling on a flat surface, which means that if we get it

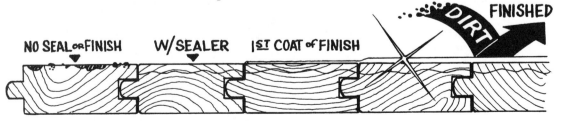

on there a little too thick it will level out. Even if you end up with some lines from your applicator or a small bubble or two, don't worry—most of these things will level out. Novices, in minutes, can lay a coat of finish that would be envied by a king and accepted by the most critical.

The Tool

Seal/finish can be put on a wood floor with several different tools.

I've tried most of the different options, and in my opinion the one made for the job is a lambswool or a short mohair type applicator—they are easiest and best. You can find both types in a paint or hardware store.

Many professionals use a weighted mohair type finish spreader. Simply pull it across the floor with a puddle of finish in front of it and it lays the finish out evenly. The weight of the applicator will allow only a certain amount to flow by and this makes for an almost perfect job.

Although these weighted applicators are getting to be the preferred choice of the pro, an amateur might find it challenging to find a place that sells or rents them. Large applicators (12"-14") are the most popular and give the best results on large floors. A roller applicator leaves bubbles and the other types of applicators are messy.

Between coats of permanent finishes you need to store the applicator pad in an air-proof plastic bag and seal it around the handle with a rubber band so your pad won't dry out. The water-based catalyst products should be washed out of the applicator with water between each coat. I usually buy one pad for the entire job and throw it away when the job is done.

Application Technique

Your goal here is to get the seal/finish on in an even, medium coat, just generous enough to fill all the wood pores. And you don't want to leave any puddles or drops or holidays (missed places). Several thin coats are better then one thick coat.

Before you apply the seal/finish to the main part of the floor, you need to do the edges. Paint the seal or finish on the edges with a regular paintbrush. Paint it out 6-8 inches from the edge, this will allow enough room for you to blend it with your main applicator. It is best to have someone paint the edges as you go, this will allow the finish to blend better. If you are alone, do a section of edges, then apply finish to the floor near that section, then more edges, more finish until the job is done. This will again prevent the picture-frame effect.

Layout

To get seal/finish out on the floor quickly, you'll get the best results pouring it out. Pour a line in the center of the area and then go back and forth across it with the applicator. When you pour, don't pour in a puddle, lay it out in rope-like stream. A puddle is hard to spread evenly.

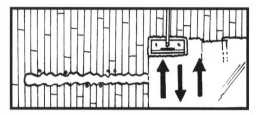

When spreading seal, always go back and forth over the same area twice to make sure it is worked into the surface, then make one final pass. But don't go back after a section is done and try to touch it up because the seal starts setting up immediately (within 3-5 minutes) and it will be sticky and you can make a mess of it. As you are spreading, look at the floor from all angles. You will inevitably see missed spots and you can get them right away. If you missed a spot in the middle of the floor, it's almost impossible to go back and get it, and on your second coat it will soak in and leave a dull spot. So as you go kneel, bend, and look at your work from different angles and light reflections to make sure you get everywhere.

Once you start, don't take a break. You always want to work from a wet edge so it will all blend together smoothly and have the same texture. If you allow a place to dry and then go back to start over, you will end up with splotches. On large floors this is more of a challenge so it is good to have an assistant. But most seals or finishes won't dry fast enough to give you any problems.

1... 2... 3... GO!

1 Pour out some seal in a stream about the size of a heavy rope. Don't overdo it! You can always pour more but it is tough to spread too much out.

NOTE: Set the container on a piece of card board to prevent the finish from running down the side of the can and causing a ring on the floor.

2 Work on about a 30-40 inch path. This is easy to reach and manage able. (I once had to have someone hold me by the belt so I could reach that last 6-8 inches when I tried to get an area that was way too wide!) Always work with a manageable area to avoid too much reaching, or stepping or falling into your new finish!

3 After the first path make the second path about the same width or smaller and continue across the floor.

4 Blend the two paths together with a lifting stroke. To do this, first work the seal/finish in with two or three passes. Then on your final stroke push and lift the applicator as you blend into the other finish. We call this feathering. If you do it right you will never leave a drag mark. The place where they meet will blend together. Too much finish on the floor will cause drips from the applicator

human slipping and sliding across it! Watch your pets, too—they will be a mess if they start skating around a newly finished floor, and so will your floor.

when you lift to feather. When dry these drips end up looking like dimes or pennies.

5 Always barricade the area with what you might consider an over kill of signs before you start. If you don't, some dork will wander across your beautiful floor and if you think a bug can botch your job, wait until you get a

---

IMPORTANT

When planning a wood floor job, allow enough time to get the job done without rushing, and leave some spare time for unforeseen problems. I talked with several contractors that have turned down jobs that would have paid a pretty penny, but had to be done in a day and a half. These contractors know they can't do a quality job under such conditions, so they pass it up.

Even the fast-drying catalyzed

products shouldn't be hurried or a poor finish results. In fact most contractors will allow the same time for the quicker drying finishes as they do for the slower drying polyure-thanes. But the quicker drying finishes usually do take considerably less time.

BETWEEN COATS

Drying time

All finishes dry at different rates. The frustrating thing is that even the manufacturers can't give an exact time frame. There are many variables—the condition of the floor, previous finishes, floor preparation, the season of the year, the moisture in the air, and how hot or cold it is, just to mention a few. Read the label. I usually go with the higher number on there. If it says six to twelve hours, I plan on twelve hours. Most important, make sure the floor is dry, not the least bit tacky before you proceed. Don't be alarmed if even after twelve hours it is still not totally set up. It might be an exceptionally humid day—don't rush it.

Wear masks for solvent base finishes.

Ventilate

Our temptation is to open every door and window in the place to get the stink out and help the finish dry faster. But the goal is to minimize the air movement to keep possible dust, debris, and insects out. Professionals close the house up tight while applying finish.

With the new water base finishes, the odor isn't as big a problem. The finish cures through a chemical reaction rather than drying.

Years ago every big job we did professionally, especially gyms, we would all go out and lay on the grass afterward to recover. The seal was absorbed into our system and we tasted and smelled it for days.

Finishes are much safer today but still require extreme caution in their use.

WARNING:

FOLLOW ALL THE DIRECTIONS!

Some products are highly flammable and can be deadly if proper precautions are not taken. I've heard some old wood refinisher stories about burning down buildings accidentally with seals and strippers. Every product is different, so read ALL label directions and FOLLOW them faithfully! If the label says no open flames that means even a pilot light on a gas stove or water heater!

Ready for the Next Coat

I've learned from years of experience that every time I tried to hurry the job along and cut out steps my end results were less desirable. A few times I had to do some major repair work because I hurried the job.

After the seal is dry, grab a red or green pad and use it on the buffer to go over the floor. Many contractors simply grab a worn 120 grit screen and screen the whole floor with it again. This does two things: First, it opens the last coat so the next coat will bond to it. Some products will bond easily to the first coat, but nothing is worse then to have the finish start peeling off in sheets. Second, it will also take any imbedded dust or hair or minor imperfections off the surface, so your next coat will be smoother.

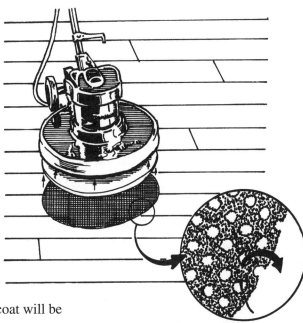

You will need to vacuum, dust, and tack the floor again before you proceed with the next coat. Tack with a cloth that is barely dampened with water. The water won't raise the grain now because the floor is sealed, and this is the safest thing to use to prevent adhesion problems.

Apply the second coat the same way you applied the first. Be careful, this will take less finish because it is not soaking into the wood. So pour our a thinner stream, than you did with the first coat.

If necessary, apply a third and fourth coat. In most cases, if you are using quality seal and finish, all that is needed is one seal coat and two permanent finish coats.

Use the same finishing technique even a year later, when applying a maintenance coat.

REMEMBER : This is a basic, general "how-to." Always read and follow the specific directions for each different seal or finish coat!

Chapter Six

The All-Important FINISH

I answer hundreds of calls and letters a month asking what to do about wood floors. The question always comes back to the finish. The importance of a good finish can't be overemphasized! I could run home right now and throw a five-gallon bucket of water on my floor and let the kids play in it without hesitation. The only reason I could do this is that I have total confidence in the finish. I know the water can't get to the wood.

To put this in perspective, the type of finish you choose will be the most important decision you will make about your wood floor. Choose the right finish and you will love your floor. The wrong choice will be a nightmare!

There are several possible scenarios and combinations of finishes, waxes, etc.

Let's start with the scenario that we have a new floor (no factory seal) or we have stripped and sanded our existing floor down to bare wood. (See Chapter Four, "Preparing a Floor for Refinishing: Sanding & Stripping.")

There are a variety of choices for wood floors, from painting to durable urethane finishes.

We will briefly discuss the pros and cons of each. When I use the word finish, it takes into account all of the following mentioned types.

The Differences Between Seal and Finish

These two terms are often used as if they were the same. As I explained in the last chapter they are not! The differences: Seals are designed as a first coat on sanded floors. They usually have a thinner, less viscous, consistency. This allows them to penetrate into wood, in fact they soak into it like a sponge. This is important to seal the wood and give a good base for the finish to adhere to.

Finishes are designed (as the name suggests) to finish the surface. Most companies have both a seal and finish product. For best results use the manufacturer's recommendation so seal and finish are compatible.

To Gloss or Not to Gloss!

When choosing a finish for your floor, you will also have to decide whether you want that surface to be a satin (dull), semigloss, or high-gloss (mirrorlike). This is personal preference. Many wood floor old-timers would turn over in their graves to see a high-gloss wood floor (but then they didn't have that option back then). Some people think a high-gloss finish makes a floor look too much like a supermarket floor. Personally, I love a high-gloss floor, but there are some considerations when choosing. The nice thing is that nowadays you do have a choice of surface type with almost any type of finish.

In my first home, I pulled up the carpet, sanded, and finished with a high-gloss finish. It knocked your eyes out! Everyone that came through the door commented on the floor. The floor was in the entry, family room, and main dining area. The first thing I did was mat the doors and entryways, but even so after a year I could see some wear showing up. I admit that as a pro I probably noticed the wear more than most people would, but eventually after two or three years it started looking like a dull no-wax floor. At that point I had to decide whether to apply acrylic polish (wax) (see Chapter Seven) or recoat my floor with a mainte-nance coat of permanent finish. Note:

When applying acrylic polish (wax) you must remember it has to be stripped before applying a maintenance coat of permanent finish in three-five years down the road.

When I moved into my new home it had satin-finished wood floors. I don't get the "WOW" comments I used to get with the high gloss, but it requires less mainte-nance and the floor always looks great, even when it's a bit dirty and worn.

My choice now is the satin (dull) or semigloss finish for my kitchen wood floor. With four children, my home seems to be the neighborhood gathering place. When the kids are older and the room has less traffic, I will probably go back to my true love, the high-gloss finish.

Both finishes are durable and if you want to take a little more time with care you can keep a high-gloss finish looking good. Visit around and look at a variety of floors and finishes in actual use before you decide.

Here's a review of the finishes available from least to most recommended:

ACRYLICS—Water Base

An acrylic polish (wax) is similar to the floor finish used on resilient tile such as in grocery stores and hospitals. Do not use this product to seal and finish bare wood, especially with the better water-based urethanes on the market. **Acrylic polish (wax) is a great maintenance product**, however, over the top of a properly finished floor. (To maintain a high-gloss all the time see Chapter Seven.)

PROS: Acrylics are quick and easy to apply, easy to remove, and easy to care for, just buff and shine, or put another coat on. They're fast drying, and a great maintenance product.

CONS: Acrylics are not a good choice for bare wood. Acrylics are poor in durability ratings, and can cause raised grain if applied to bare wood. They are also not very chemical resistant, and this can cause adhesion problems for a refinisher or with maintenance coats if they aren't compatible.

OIL—Danish, Swedish, Tung Oil

Oils were used to finish wood floors years ago because they were cheap and their rich, deep, matte finish was the desired look. Now only old homes that are being restored to their original flavor, museums, etc., desire an oil look. (Note: This look can be achieved with other, easier-to-maintain finishes, too.)

PROS: The look of elegance.

CONS: Oil offers only minimal protection from wear and moisture. It is a high-maintenance finish and often requires paste wax and constant buffing. Oil also limits options for sanding and refinishing.

VARNISH

There is not much call for varnish anymore with the polyurethanes available. There are a few old-timers out there who still think it is the toughest stuff and the only thing for wood.

PROS: Tough, durable finish.

CONS: Slow drying, darkens and yellows considerably with age.

Although the mainstay for years, it has all but been totally replaced with better finishes.

POLYURETHANES
(Oil modified/solvent)

These were the most widely used finishes until a couple years ago. There are several companies that sell a wood floor finish by a specific brand name, but it could be just a plain old polyurethane. Polyurethanes have proven to be one of the toughest finishes on the market. Unlike the old varnishes, polyurethanes are clear and remain clear. Varnishes would yellow and darken to a dark brown in five or ten years. Floors coated with polyurethane can have several maintenance coats without getting darker.

PROS: Polyurethanes are fairly easy to use and the cost is reasonable. They are easy to obtain and give professional results. Great for maintenance coats.

CONS: Polyurethanes are flammable, and have an unpleasant odor during application and drying.

Drying time is six to eight hours; ultimate cure time is seven days.

WATERTHANES

Waterthanes are similar to the polyurethanes on the market, except they use water as the carrier instead of solvents. We see this in paints, there are both water base and oil base. Waterthanes are a blend of polyurethanes and acrylics. The polyurethane gives the finish durability and the acrylic adds workability to the finish and also helps it level out.

PROS: Waterthanes are non-smelly, nonflammable, and easy to apply. Cleanup is fast with water and no dangerous solvents. Waterthanes dry fast and have a great leveling ability too. Great for quick do-it-yourselfers.

CONS: Waterthanes do not penetrate and seal (first coat) wood well, and they cause raised grain on the first coat. And they are only medium on the durability scale.

Don't confuse waterthanes with acrylic polish (wax) water-base products.

CATALYZED FINISHES

(Water Base)

Catalyzed finishes are a relatively new concept in wood floor finishes. These products are similar to polyurethanes, in that they are as durable as the solvent-based polyurethanes, but are as safe and easy to use as the waterthanes. The difference is that the gallon of finish has a 3-4 oz. bottle of catalyst that is mixed into the product before application and it cures by chemical reaction rather than evaporation like water or solvent.

PROS: A catalyzed finish is very durable, fairly easy to apply, has little objectionable odor, is nonflammable and fast-drying. Ultimate cure time is two hours.

CONS: The catalyzed finish is high

cost—$50 to $80 a gallon. Recoating options are limited. There are two parts that require mixing. The catalyst itself is a hazardous chemical.

Two years ago I would not have recommended a catalyst finish, but today, the larger companies have all but perfected this product. Many contractors are moving to this and many use it exclusively.

POLYURETHANES
(Water-base Oxygen Crosslinked)

We often see innovation forced by environmental concerns. The wood floor industry has come a long way not only in the way trees are harvested but in the types and durability of finishes. New to the market, the last couple of years is a 100% polyurethane water base product. The chemists have developed a curing (chemical reaction) agent that when exposed to air acts as a cross linked catalyst. This means we can get the same durability without any additives. These are a little tougher to find, contact wood floor installers or contractors. They haven't hit the mainstream home improvement stores yet. These finishes are taking over the industry for good reason.

PROS: Has a low odor (VOC compliant) needs little ventilation. No hazardous additives. One of the most durable finishes. Easy to apply. Fast drying.

CONS: Hard to find. Still a little costly.

OTHER FINISHES

There are other finishes out there that are very specialized. If you are reading this book you don't even want to know about them. The point is, these are oil modified moisture cure acid modified urethanes with an alcohol base. Some are harder to apply or have special handling considerations. Most manufacturer won't sell these to anyone except a certified floor contractor. Stay away from these products. Also stay away from products that might have been on someone's shelf for a long time or a old gym finish that no one knows much about. Finish products have come a long way in just the last few years and "bargain stock" might be out of date or experimental stuff.

PRE-FINISHED

Most all Pre-finished floors are ultraviolet-cured polyurethane. After the wood is prepared, the finish is applied by spray or roller and put through a curing booth in which UV light instantly cures the finish. This process is repeated several times to get the desired number of coats. It is a strong and hardy finish. This finish cannot be applied by contractors or installers on site, but it is a growing part of the market and will be a buying choice you will be offered.

PROS: With a UV finish, only installation of the wood itself is required. Each board has an even application of very durable finish, and a maintenance coat can be applied, the wood can be recoated with polyurethane when needed.

CONS: Pre-finished wood is susceptible to moisture getting between the boards and some floor designs and options are not available.

THE BOTTOM LINE

The finish industry is on a fast track to find safe, durable, easy-to-use, environmentally friendly products. Their products have come a long way in the last five years.

For the do-it-yourselfer, I would only consider two finishes, polyurethane (oil modified) or oxygen crosslinked polyurethane. The results are about the same when it comes to durability, appearance, finish care, etc. If I had to choose *today*, I would opt for the new oxygen crosslinked polyurethane. It is a tad more expensive and harder to find, and though catalyzed products are applied in the same manner, there is a time constraint and special mixing requirements. The cost of oil modified polyurethane is often a third as much as catalyzed finish and the quality of the end result is as good, so there is a savings there.

Overall it is almost impossible to mess up the new oxygen crosslinked polyurethane. There are some considerations to bear in mind, however, the smell and flammability of the product being paramount. If these are a big factor for environmental reasons (in some areas solvent-based products aren't available or are very scarce), you might want to pass on polyurethane. Drying time is also a consideration—with the new products you can shorten the time needed. Professionals often plan on the same amount of time regardless of the finish. They say the biggest problem with do-it-yourselfers is they plan it like a paint job. But if your wood floor refinishing runs late, you *CAN'T* finish it the next weekend. You have to complete the job once you start it.

Chapter Seven

Cleaning and Maintaining Wood Floors

Every time I do seminars, speaking engagements, home shows, etc., those wood floor questions keep coming up. Plus I answer several phone calls a week about wood floors, and I always hear the same question: "How do I clean my wood floor?" The answer comes down to: what condition is the floor in and what kind of finish is on it?

It is impossible to prescribe a solution without knowing these things.

REGULAR/DAILY CARE

All floors need regular care, regardless of their style, color, or whether they are tile, rock, carpet, vinyl, or wood! In all of our professional experience we have found that maintenance is the key to preserving and extending the life of floors, especially carpets and wood floors, and keeping them looking great longer.

REMEMBER: Chapter One is what gives us the foundation to go on, DON'T SKIP IT! This chapter will diagnose your situation and from there we can prescribe the cure. (There I go sounding like the wood floor doctor again!)

De-dirting

Regularly remove all dirt, dust, dry soil, and family fallout from the surface of the floor. It's simple, but this alone can make all the difference. Get rid of the daily accumulation on your floor—the dust, dropped food, and grit tracked in from outside—before it has a chance to be ground in. Wood can camouflage so well it is easy to ignore the dirt. Don't let it build up until it's noticeable, de-dirt often. You have some choices as to how to go about this. Pick the one of that will fit your schedule and style, and not take much time.

CHOOSE YOUR TOOL

SWEEP

If you choose to sweep, using a broom that can and will pick up even the "fine stuff" is a must. The old corn brooms are okay, but not as good as the new plastic brooms with exploded ends (split tips) to get dust and fine grit.

VACUUM

Probably the surest way to get every bit of the dust and dirt is with a vacuum.

Don't use an upright vacuum with a beater bar or roller brushes, they can cause damage to a wood floor. Other than that your options here are many. If you have a built-in (central) vacuum or are thinking of getting one, they work great! They usually have a floor tool made for wood floors.

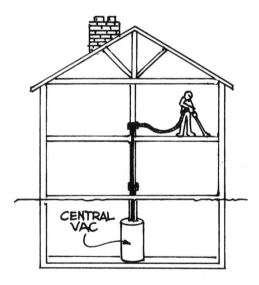

Canister vacuums are also well suited for the job because they are suction only. The Eureka Mighty Mite compact cannister vac with a floor tool also works wonderfully. Most canisters have a bare floor tool with soft hair bristles and this is what you want to have. You **don't** want to use the "power head" or "power wand" of a canister vac, because these, again, contain roller brushes. Another vacuum-type tool I've used is the Super Broom by Eureka. It costs about $60 and is quick and handy and works great on wood floors with area rugs.

Vacuuming can be more time-consuming on small areas and quicker on large areas, but once you get that machine out of the closet, it is the most effective way of getting up the dust and debris. And you won't have to grab the dustpan and sweep up the pile! Just be sure to vacuum the whole floor, not just the obvious dirt you can see.

DUST MOP

This is the professional choice for large areas of hard flooring, especially wood. You may have seen these at high-school ball games when the pro cleaners bring out those six-foot mops at half time. Dust mopping is second only to vacuuming in effectiveness and is much easier and quicker overall.

Pick a good dust mop, don't waste your time on the twinky ones you find in the grocery store. They aren't any better than a broom.

A dust mop with an eighteen-inch head is the best size for most large wood floors at home. For medium to small areas I use the Scrubbee Doo tool (see page 78) with a twelve-inch dust mop head that attaches with Velcro-like teeth to the bottom of the tool. This is great because when it gets dirty, just peel it off and throw it in the wash!

Dust Mop Treatment

Dust mops must be treated to do their best. Dust mops alone aren't any better than a rolled up bath towel, they will just push the dirt and dust around. The magic of a treated dust mop is that it acts like a magnet, grabbing and holding on to dust, dirt, and debris. And it will keep holding onto that dust and dirt until you shake it off. Spray the head with a good coat of dust treatment, wrap it in a plastic bag, then leave it over-night. This gives the treatment time to penetrate the fibers.

The manufacturers of some wood floor finishes discourage the use of dust mops because of the oil treatment, but if a mop is treated correctly it will not leave any residue on the floor. There are also water-based treatments on the market. They perform about the same and will make some of the skeptics happier.

Retreat the mop every month or so. Don't worry if it gets a bit grungy—dust mops seem to work even better when broken in. Once the head gets unbearable throw it into the washer and dryer and it will come out like new.

A dust mop is designed to be used in a figure-eight motion. Don't push and sweep like a broom. Keep the head of the mop on the floor at all times. Imagine you are trying to keep a marble or a bunch of BB's moving ahead of you.

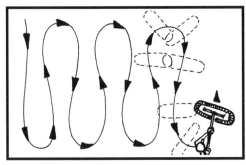

Pick a spot for a pile. When doing a large floor you will need to stop and shake off the dust and dirt a couple of times in the course of your dust mopping.

Now grab your counter broom and dustpan and pick the dirt up. If you have a vacuum handy, quickly vacuum it up. Vacuum the dust mop head off occasionally. This keeps it in great shape and the fine dust in control.

Whichever method you choose, make regular maintenance a habit. The location of your wood floor has a lot to do with how often you will need to de-dirt. I sweep or vacuum my kitchen every day, and my entryway at least once a week (I've got good door mats down). I do my dining room every couple of weeks (we only eat Sunday dinner there). The beauty of a wood floor is worth a little extra effort.

WHEN IT DOES GET DIRTY

Yes, it will eventually get dirty. But you knew that! I've actually had some people tell me that they have never cleaned their wood floor. With four kids, I can't even fathom this—I know how my floor would look!

I've seen "experts" break into a sweat when asked how to clean a wood floor. Most installers will tell you to ask someone else—a manufacturer, distributor, or retailer, they try to pass the buck to someone else, or make you feel like a weirdo for having a dirty floor. You won't have to ask anymore because here is the answer.

MOP IT

The best way to clean hard floors is by mopping, using practically the same process you would on any other floor. I will describe that shortly.

What Solution Do I Use?

A number of floor manufacturers recommend mopping with plain water, or a favorite buzz word is "vinegar." Vinegar is probably the worst advice out there. At the last National Wood Floor Convention I attended I acted dumb and asked everyone what I should use to clean my wood floor—60-70% told me vinegar. I asked "Why vinegar," and they came back with several answers, none of which made much sense. Vinegar isn't a cleaner, it doesn't get the grease, dried milk, or mud, the smeared jam and squashed raisins, or the Jello, potato, and hot dog pieces (I'm going by what I find on my floor at home). No matter how hard you try to keep your floor spotless, something is always going to get on it. Vinegar can't really hurt anything and it's fine as a rinsing agent. When added to rinse water it doesn't leave a soap film and that is why some people like it.

But if you try to clean with vinegar the gunk will still be there. Cleaning is the process of using a solution to release soil. If you use the right solution it will float the soil to the surface where it can be removed easily and quickly with a cloth or mop.

Wood floors are no different than any other floor, they encounter the same kinds of soil. In the kitchen, for instance, cooking grease is all over—run your finger across the top of the refrigerator, that stuff is on the floor, too, it's just hiding in the grain. It's a mixture of dust, dirt, and grease. On the floor we also get food smears and spills, and footwear fallout.

Cleaners are rated on the pH scale. High pH cleaners are alkaline and work better on grease, oil, smoke, and stubborn soil. Low pH cleaners are acidic and work on hard water deposits and mineral scale. The higher the pH, the faster and more effective a cleaner usually is, but a high pH cleaner also has a greater chance of damaging the surface of the finish and a super high pH is dangerous to human skin. The key is to find a cleaner that will release the soil without dulling the surface you are cleaning. For wood floors this means a neutral cleaner, Top Sheen or Wood Wash. These are mild, safe cleaners that work well, and this is what you should look for. These cleaners are called "neutral cleaners" because they have a neutral pH, they are neither acid or alkaline.

I use a product called Wood Wash, a professional product specially formulated for wood and wood finishes. In the store look for a product that claims to be mild and neutral. Stay away from the so-called wood cleaners with vegetable oil or oil soaps in them, they leave a film and residue. Some cleaners have waxes in them and can cause havoc when you have to put on a maintenance coat of finish.

A simple solution of 2-4 oz. of Wood Wash or neutral cleaner to a gallon of water is all you need for mopping and cleaning of wood floors. Many floor manufacturers and even finish brands recommend their own brand of cleaners to go with their product. Most specialized cleaners sold by the manufacturers of the finish are nothing special and don't need to be use. Don't worry if they say you will void the warranty.

ONLY 2 OUNCES

WOOD WASH

1 gal. water

Wood Soaps

Most wood soaps claim to be miracle cleaners and preservatives for wood. Most have some type of oily ingredient (such as vegetable oil) which tends to build up on the surface of the finish and become sticky. Stay away from soaps that claim to be all in one. Most are okay cleaners, but the oils and other ingredients aren't necessary here and will defeat your purpose.

"Waterless Cleaners"

I would avoid these unless you are dealing with bare wood with no finish (which is very rare). Most are solvent based (smells like paint thinner). They will clean, but not as effectively as soap and water and with repeated use they start to deteriorate the finish. If wood is sealed correctly there is no need for these. They are expensive and potentially dangerous.

If all else fails,
READ THE DIRECTIONS!

Using too much cleaner concentrate in your bucket can be as bad as not using enough. Cleaner molecules are designed to grab on to the dirt molecules. When too much cleaner is used the dirt gets swept away but the excess cleaner hangs around and this is what causes a residue or film. The manufacturers of cleaners have a very good idea of how their product performs. All cleaners come in different concentrations and require different dilutions, so follow the directions!

MOP

The size of the floor is a factor here. If you have one or two small areas a sponge mop (buy a professional-quality one) will be plenty. For larger areas or high-traffic floors buy a string mop. For home use buy a small to medium size, 12-16 oz. You will need a wringer bucket with this and buy a good one. This setup will cost you $50-$100, but it is worth the extra bucks up front. Professional-quality supplies like these can usually be found in a janitorial supply store or from the Cleaning Center (see pages 77-80).

For medium to small areas I use a mopping pad called a Quick Mop on a Scrubbee Doo (a long-handled floor scrubber with a swivel scrubbing head). This is great for quick mopping or cleaning up spills, and I am using it more and more for all my mopping chores. I often use it directly out of the sink. The only drawback is that you have to wring it out by hand. Use rubber gloves and it won't be so dreadful.

HOW TO MOP

There are two basic types of mopping, damp-mopping or quick mopping, and heavy-duty mopping.

Damp-Mopping

If you sweep regularly, clean up spills immediately, and damp-mop often, this will be all you need to do. It is only when you let a floor go that you need to deep down (heavy-duty) mop.

To damp-mop start by getting the mop wet in the cleaning solution and then wring it out about half dry. Now go over

CHOOSE YOUR MOP TOOL:

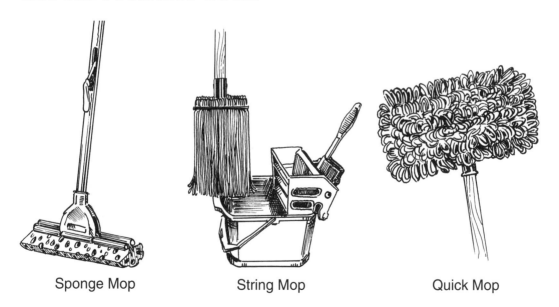

Sponge Mop   String Mop   Quick Mop

the floor or area once to dampen it. The first trip over you are simply wetting the floor, covering the surface with cleaner. It will attack the soil and loosen it. Now dip the mop back into the solution or plain water and wring it as dry as possible and go back over the floor—"WOW!" It picks

up the dirt suspended in the solution.

In most cases there is no need to rinse the floor if the proper cleaner is used in the proper dilution. Some people will grab a cleaning terrycloth and completely dry the floor. This is a good safety, but not necessary if you have a good finish.

This is the safest and best way to maintain wood floors, and it will work on any finish. Used this way, water won't penetrate even the oil finishes.

Light Scrubbing, Heavy-Duty Mopping or Deep Cleaning

This requires a little more water and more "dwell time" (the amount of time the cleaner is left on the floor surface to work) and maybe a little scrubbing. Even here, if your floor is sealed properly, you have nothing to worry about.

Dip your mop in the solution and wring it only slightly. Use the same solution as for damp-mopping, and if soil is built up use a little higher percentage of

cleaner to water, but don't get carried away—a little cleaner can do a lot of good. Spread the solution on the floor, working in 12'x12' sections at a time (often this will be half the floor.) Then grab a white or blue nylon scrub pad and give the area a scrub with a Scrubbee Doo. This will help release any stubborn spots or soil. Now wring the mop completely dry (as dry as you can get it) and mop up the solution. When you're done dip the mop in solution or clear water and wring it dry and go over the area again. Continue the same way across the floor. If the floor is extra dirty grab an extra bucket and use it to rinse the mop out, to avoid dirtying the cleaning solution.

Heavy-duty mopping is another RED FLAG with the wood floor people. When we say spread water on the floor, they are afraid we will dump gallons out on it. Just use some common sense here. Use enough solution to wet the floor, but not to saturate it. Also, here we come back again to the integrity of the finish: if you have a good finish on your floor you could build a swimming pool on it!

Now that the floor is back in shape, continue to damp-mop on a regular basis at least once a week. This will delay or prevent the need for future deep cleaning.

QUICK CLEANUP!

Remember, REGULAR MAINTE-NANCE is the KEY to easy floor care!

SPILLS–Keep your eyes open for spills. I can almost guarantee that after the kids eat I will find things under the table that require a quick pickup—crushed Cheerios, Jello, gum, Kool-Aid, you name it. Keep a dozen terry cleaning cloths handy in the kitchen and get the spills when they happen.

I keep a spray bottle with neutral cleaning solution on hand and when I need to touch up between moppings I simply spray the area and go over it once

with a cleaning cloth on the bottom of my Scrubbee Doo tool to mop up any soil. This leaves it almost dry. Fast and simple!

Acrylic Polish (wax)
To Wax or Not to Wax?

Does it seem that there are many "do nots" and very few "dos" when it comes to wood floor care?

Wax is another one of those controversial subjects, at least when you talk to people in the wood floor industry. Wax to them sounds like an illegal drug. Professional cleaners, on the other hand, use acrylic polish (wax) on almost everything. It is a necessity to keep floors that get hard use looking good, and we professional cleaners can't get along without it on hard-surface floors in commercial buildings.

If you asked a wood floor retailer about wax he would tell you that you never need to wax because the surface is like a no-wax surface.

The installers and refinishers tell you never to use wax because if they come back to recoat the floor with finish someday that wax can cause adhesion problems. They will tell you that waxing a floor will cause the floor to have to be sanded before it can be recoated. This doesn't sound good for wax, but wax does have its place on wood floors.

First, if you have a new floor with a good finish on it (a number "4 or 5" on our chart in Chapter One), leave the finish as long as possible. Don't put a coat of acrylic polish (wax) over the finish to protect it, the finish is usually more durable than the wax and will hold up better in the long run. When it gets dull

you have to decide to wax with acrylic polish or to apply a maintenance coat of permanent finish.

When to Wax

The majority of people who call me about their wood floors don't want to spend the time or money to sand and refinish. They just want their floor to look good without all that trouble. Acrylic polish (wax) is the answer.

A good maintenance program that includes acrylic polish (wax) is also the answer if you are super picky and want a floor to look immaculate all the time.

Don't let the retailer, installer or refinisher scare you to death when you mention wax. Most of the true experts (who keep wood floors looking great) use acrylic polish (wax) on 90% of the floors they maintain. Even though acrylic polish (wax) will mean stripping down the road.

Acrylic polish (wax) is the most workable beauty treatment for wood floors. It can be cleaned, buffed, and rewaxed, and the floor can be restored to

its original glory in a matter of half an hour. In most cases I recommend applying it on top of seals and finishes.

The advantage of wax is that when it's on there all the wear and tear will be on the wax and not on the finish of the floor. Wax can easily be removed or stripped off and new wax applied. You can maintain the beauty of the floor without being 100% dependent on the condition of the finish.

The only reason not to wax your floor is if you are going to recoat it with finish sometime soon. If a floor has been waxed and not properly stripped before recoating, it can cause an adhesion problem (and this causes the refinisher sleepless nights when he or she has the job of refinishing your floor).

If I were going to recoat a polyurethane floor, I would almost always use a wax remover/degreaser before I proceeded to screen the floor. Some installers/refinishers don't think you can get all the wax off just by stripping it. I've never had an adhesion problem doing this but maybe I've just been lucky.

There are a variety of acrylic polishes (waxes) available, here is a brief description of the two main types:

Acrylic Polish (Wax)

These liquid water-base waxes are used almost everywhere–hospitals, supermarkets, malls, homes. Different grades are available, based on their "solids" content. Solids are the plasticizers and polymers that remain on the surface of the floor after the wax dries. Waxes bought in supermarkets are 8-12% solids. Cheaper commercial waxes are 16-19% solids. The best waxes are 21-29% solids. The higher the solids content, the more durable, long-lasting, and scuff resistant a wax is. Of course, the high-solids waxes are more expensive, but outlast the cheap waxes 10 to 1, and have a better gloss and appearance.

Pick a high-solids wax like Top Gloss or ask for a high-solids wax at a janitorial supply store. This is the stuff they would give you if you just walked in and ask for a commercial wax.

PASTE WAX

As the name implies, this is indeed a pasty substance. Paste wax is similar to paste shoe polish. Most paste waxes are made of carnauba, a true wax from trees in Brazil that is also found in the

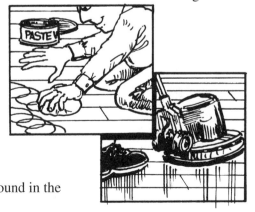

most expensive car waxes. Paste wax is usually solvent rather than water-based.

Paste wax is a great way to go if you want a satin finish. It also requires much more work than the acrylic waxes. It is applied to the floor and buffed in with a fine steel wool or a medium coarse buffing pad. This lays the wax down and picks up most of the dirt and debris. For best results the floor should be cleaned before waxing.

WAXED FLOOR MAINTENANCE

A brilliant glossy supermarket floor is a trophy to the industry. Most people don't know the maintenance required to keep it looking like that.

Even at home, once we have waxed our floor, proper maintenance is required to keep it looking great. Even the shiniest surface will start to dull after use, and then we need to rewax. Simply scrub the floor with a neutral pH cleaner like Top Sheen or Wood Wash (see page 80), then rinse and recoat. Recoat only the traffic areas unless the entire floor is dull. Maintain a waxed floor the same as the original finish.

Lights! Camera! Action!

The last floor I refinished was last summer for the filming of my television "Clean in a Minute" segments. There was a wood floor in the basement of an old apartment house, we yanked up the rug and there it was! The television crew was fascinated with the process and captivated by the end result. Let me just walk you through the job, which by the way, was completed (floor and film) in four hours! This was a 12' x 12' room the size of a medium bedroom.

Take One - 11:30 am

We pulled up the carpet and right then hauled it out and away from the area. TOSS IT right now! It is full of grit and dust, many of us just get it out of the way somewhere and then start moving it while the seal is drying and really foul things up.

We swept and vacuumed then to remove any mess (so we

wouldn't be grinding in any gravel, sand, grit, etc.) before we removed the tack strip.

Take Two - 12:00 n

We popped up the tack strip. A flat bar with a curved end works fast and is wide enough so it won't bruise the wood. Use gloves, there are at least a thousand needle sharp nails in these. Have a cardboard box right with

you to put them in, don't carry them in your arms etc. There will be small "A" holes in the wood floor afterward from the fastening nail of the tack strip. Don't worry about them they never show much. If you do want to fill them the best time is now, with some wood putty that matches the basic

color of the wood. After removing the tack strips we swept again.

12:30 pm

We went and got a bite to eat. The camera crew didn't want to work though lunch.

Take Three - 1:10 pm

I took two minutes and wiped the entire floor down with mineral spirits (paint thinner). This showed me where the worn

spots and stains were. There were a couple of bad spots that would need extra attention when screening.

Take Four

I put a walkoff mat next to the floor and opened a window and turned a fan out the window to blow any screening dust outside, instead of letting it settle on everything inside.

Take Five - 1:20 pm

We started screening now using both types of floor machines. The oscillator type works like a hand sander only bigger. It has no torque so it is easy to control. It is slower, but easier and safer.

The rotary type sander is a plain old buffer or floor machine, really fast and heavier than the oscillator. It can be difficult to control the swinging motion on this.

We used both to show the differences, but ended up using the buffer to finish the job.

Screening was simple. We worked in large areas, changing the screen when needed. We were sanding the edges with a belt sander at the same time.

After the finish was removed, we quickly went over the floor with a finer screen.

Take Six

We kept it vacuumed to see our progress and to keep the dust down. It was dusty! When we got to the trouble spots or stains I grabbed a cloth dampened with mineral spirits and wiped the

area. This gave us an idea of how the floor would look sealed.

Step Seven - 3:30 pm

The floor was bare and ready to be sealed. We did final preparation by vacuuming again and

using a tack rag to pick up any dust.

3:30 pm

We applied the first coat of seal. It only took fifteen minutes. I used a lambswool applicator and then just threw it away.

4:00 pm

We were finished. The floor had to dry and we put a second coat on two days later. Most floors can be recoated after 12-20 hours and some even sooner.

It Was That Easy!

It is hard to imagine you could refinish a wood floor in an afternoon! Most think this was a week long project. You don't need to take your vacation to do it!

Professional Equipment & Supplies

MATS
(indoor and outdoor)

The #1 preventive! 2'x3', or 3'x4' are the most common house-hold sizes, but they can be purchased in almost any size. Buy them long enough for at least two strides. AstroTurf for outside all entrances—even the garage! Nylon or olefin fiber on vinyl or rubber backing for inside. Help keep dust, grit and other debris from being tracked in and absorb water from foot traffic. Available from janitorial supply stores or from the Cleaning Center.

CLEANING CLOTH

Made from 18"x18" piece of cotton terrycloth. Sewn into a "tube." Replaces the "rag." Can be used for most cleaning jobs. By folding and turning inside out there are *16* cleaning surfaces. Make them yourself or order from the Cleaning Center.

SPRAY
BOTTLE

Quart spray bottle, plastic with professional-quality trigger sprayer. Fill with diluted neutral cleaner for spot cleaning floors or other general cleaning duties. Keep several around the house in convenient locations. Available at janitorial supply stores or from the Cleaning Center.

DUSTMOP

Dustmop with 18" or 24" cotton head and rotating handle. For use on all hard floors. Fast and efficient; lasts for years. Use dust treatment for best results. Shake out and vacuum head regularly; launder when dirt-saturated, then pretreat. Available at janitorial supply stores or from the Cleaning Center.

DUSTMOP
TREATMENT

To use with your new dustmop. This specially formulated aerosol is used to treat the dustmop to hold every bit of dust and dirt. Can also be used to treat dust cloths. Spray directly on dustmop or cloth and let it sit overnight to penetrate the fibers.

SCRUBBEE DOO

Long-handled floor scrubber with three 5"x10" nylon scrub pads. For effortless scrubbing of hard floors—even concrete (cleans almost anything—showers, baseboards, glass, too). Comes with three different strength pads for light, medium, and heavy-duty scrubbing. Pads easily peel off the Velcro-like teeth. Additional pads for different jobs available, see below. Available at janitorial supply stores or from the Cleaning Center.

DUSTMOP PAD

Made exclusively to attach to Scrubbee Doo swivel floor tool. Professional quality, better than a broom on small to large wood and tile floors. Use with dustmop treatment; washable. Available from the Cleaning Center.

QUICK MOP PAD

Made exclusively to attach to Scrubbee Doo swivel floor tool. Mopping pad for quick clean up, great for damp mopping small to medium size floors. Washable. Available from the Cleaning Center.

WAX APPLICATOR PAD

Made exclusively to attach to Scrubbee Doo swivel floor tool. Professional results every time. Use to apply any type of finish, from waxes to concrete seal. Washable. Available from the Cleaning Center.

WAX APPLICATOR

Long-handled applicator with a head that is usually a block of wood with lambswool or simulated fleece wrapped around it, for a smooth, even finish. Available at paint and hardware stores.

For more information call the Cleaning Center 800-451-2402.

STRING MOP & WRINGER BUCKET

12 oz., 16 oz., or large 24 oz. rayon/cotton; Screw-type handle enables heads to be replaced easily. A 4-gallon plastic bucket with self-contained roller wringer. When you damp mop, the self contained wringer saves injuries from hand-wringing. For damp-mopping if you have a great deal of hard flooring. Available at janitorial supply stores or from the Cleaning Center.

ANGLE BROOM

Professional–quality plastic broom with split-tip nylon bristles for quick cleanups, sweeping small areas, and doing edges and corners before vacuuming or dustmopping. Available at janitorial supply stores or from the Cleaning Center.

SQUARE BUFFER

A large buffer that works like an oscillating hand sander. It is easier to handle than the rotating buffer but may be harder to find and rent. Good for getting edges. Also from rental shops.

BUFFER

Rotating floor machine, from rental shops. Get a demonstration when renting and try it out, it is tricky to use but easy to learn to operate. Heavily used in commercial cleaning for scrubbing, stripping, and polishing.

SCREENS & DISKS

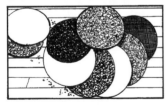

Screens are found in several different grits from 30 to 200. Used to remove finish and sand a wood floor. Used also to final touch up before a finish is applied. Disks are made of material similar to regular sand paper. The heavier grits in disks such as 30-60 tend to work better than the heavier grits in screens. Available at janitorial supply stores and rental shops.

HAND SANDER

Small hand-held, oscillating sander. Great for edges and corners. Can use either screen or sandpaper material on it. Hardware department, or rental store.

CANISTER VACUUM
Mighty Mite

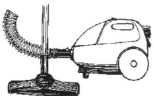

There are two options—the larger one is designed with a power nozzle for complete floor care, carpet, wood floors plus other household jobs. The compact canister is designed to get all the tough jobs, stairs, edges, upholstery, autos, etc., usually doesn't come with an electric power nozzle, this is a great combination with an upright vacuum. Available at janitorial supply stores or from the Cleaning Center.

WET/DRY VACUUM

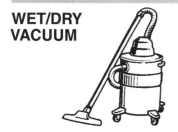

10-gallon metal or plastic tank. Be sure you get one with a rust-resistant tank. And get squeegee, upholstery and edge tool attachments with it. Can be used like a canister vacuum for all household vacuuming, as well as to pick up water when scrubbing floors, or to pick up spills and overflows. Widely available at discount, hardware, or janitorial supply stores.

NEUTRAL CLEANER

TOP SHEEN OR WOOD WASH! Concentrated in quart or gallon size. Dilute as directed for mopping or spray-and-wipe cleaning. This is the best product to clean your floors. A neutral cleaner won't leave a residue or dull a waxed surface. Safe for all types of floors. Won't damage household surfaces or remove floor wax/finish. Available from the Cleaning Center.

MOP STRIPPER

Non-ammoniated, quart or gallon size. Professional power to remove old wax and dirt buildup without scraping. It will get in all the pits and grooves and need very little scrubbing; turns old wax into liquid so it can be mopped up. Designed to take off most commercial finishes, so household wax buildup is no problem. Available from the Cleaning Center.

TOP GLOSS
Acrylic Polish (Wax)

Quart or gallon size, metal interlock self-polishing. Top Gloss protects all hard floor surfaces—wood, tile, linoleum, sealed concrete and no-wax floors, also used on wood floors to maintain a high gloss. A quart covers 200 square feet; a gallon covers 800 square feet. Available from the Cleaning Center.

For more information call the Cleaning Center 800-451-2402.

CLEANING!:

Don Aslett
America's No.1 Cleaning Expert
Is There Life After Housework?

Don Aslett's CLEAN IN A MINUTE

PET CLEAN-UP MADE EASY
America's #1 Cleaning Expert and bestselling author of Is There Life After Housework? and Clutter's Last Stand
Don Aslett

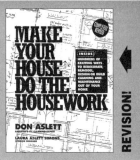
MAKE YOUR HOUSE DO THE HOUSEWORK
INSIDE: HUNDREDS OF EXCITING WAYS TO REDECORATE, REMODEL, DESIGN OR BUILD CLEANING AND MAINTENANCE OUT OF YOUR HOME
DON ASLETT
AMERICA'S #1 CLEANING EXPERT
LAURA ASLETT SIMONS INTERIOR DESIGNER

REVISION!

CLUTTER:

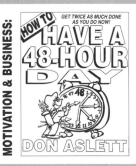
CLUTTER'S LAST STAND
by Don Aslett
America's #1 Cleaning Expert
It's time to De-Junk your life!

HOW TO CLEAN UP, CLEAR OUT, AND DEJUNK YOUR LIFE FOREVER!
NOT FOR PACKRATS ONLY
DON ASLETT
Author of HOW DO I CLEAN THE MOOSEHEAD? and CLUTTER'S LAST STAND

THE OFFICE CLUTTER CURE
How to get out from under it all!
DON ASLETT
AMERICA'S #1 DEJUNKER

DON ASLETT'S CLUTTER FREE! Finally & Forever
Including true confessions & solutions from 100's of your fellow packrats.

MORE MAINTENANCE:

DON ASLETT'S STAINBUSTER'S BIBLE
THE COMPLETE GUIDE TO SPOT REMOVAL

500 TERRIFIC IDEAS FOR CLEANING EVERYTHING
Expert Advice to Take You from Choosing & Using Supplies to Cleaning Absolutely Everything—Faster & More Effectively
Don Aslett

The CLEANING ENCYCLOPEDIA
Your A to Z Illustrated guide to cleaning like the pros!
Don Aslett

WHO SAYS IT'S A WOMAN'S JOB TO CLEAN?
by **DON ASLETT**

MOTIVATION & BUSINESS:

HOW TO HAVE A 48-HOUR DAY
GET TWICE AS MUCH DONE AS YOU DO NOW!
DON ASLETT

EVERYTHING I NEEDED TO KNOW ABOUT **BUSINESS** I LEARNED IN THE **BARNYARD!**
THE BUSINESS BASICS HANDBOOK BY **DON ASLETT**

How to be #1 with your Boss
How to keep your job longer & enjoy it more.
DON ASLETT

Don Aslett's You can... You should... Write Poetry
POETRY

PROFESSIONAL CLEANERS:

From America's #1 Cleaning Expert
CLEANING UP FOR A LIVING
2nd Edition
Don A. Aslett
Mark L. Browning
Everything you need to know to become a successful building service contractor.

THE Professional CLEANER'S HANDBOOK
DON ASLETT

How to UPGRADE and MOTIVATE Your Cleaning Crews
by DON ASLETT

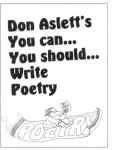
Don Aslett's Professional Cleaner's CLIP ART

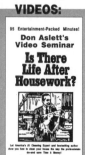

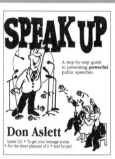

CLEANING!:

Don Aslett
America's No. 1 Cleaning Expert
Is There *Life* After Housework?

Don Aslett's
CLEAN IN A MINUTE

PET CLEAN-UP MADE EASY
Don Aslett

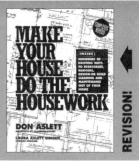

MAKE YOUR HOUSE DO THE HOUSEWORK
DON ASLETT
LAURA ASLETT SIMONS

REVISION!

CLUTTER:

CLUTTER'S LAST STAND
by Don Aslett
America's #1 Cleaning Expert
It's time to De-Junk your life!

HOW TO CLEAN UP, CLEAR OUT, AND DEJUNK YOUR LIFE FOREVER!
NOT FOR PACKRATS ONLY
DON ASLETT

THE OFFICE CLUTTER CURE
How to get out from under it all!
DON ASLETT

DON ASLETT'S CLUTTER FREE!
Finally & Forever
Including true confessions & solutions from 100's of your fellow packrats.

MORE MAINTENANCE:

DON ASLETT'S STAINBUSTER'S BIBLE
THE COMPLETE GUIDE TO SPOT REMOVAL

500 TERRIFIC IDEAS FOR CLEANING EVERYTHING
Don Aslett

The CLEANING ENCYCLOPEDIA
Your A to Z illustrated guide to cleaning like the pros!
Don Aslett

WHO SAYS IT'S A WOMAN'S JOB TO CLEAN?
by DON ASLETT

MOTIVATION & BUSINESS:

GET TWICE AS MUCH DONE AS YOU DO NOW!
HOW TO HAVE A 48-HOUR DAY
DON ASLETT

EVERYTHING I NEEDED TO KNOW ABOUT BUSINESS I LEARNED IN THE BARNYARD!
THE BUSINESS BASICS HANDBOOK BY DON ASLETT

How to be #1 with your Boss
How to keep your job longer & enjoy it more.
DON ASLETT

Don Aslett's
You can...
You should...
Write Poetry

PROFESSIONAL CLEANERS:

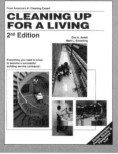

From America's #1 Cleaning Expert
CLEANING UP FOR A LIVING
2nd Edition
Don A. Aslett
Mark L. Browning
Everything you need to know to become a successful building service contractor.

THE Professional CLEANER'S HANDBOOK
DON ASLETT

How to UPGRADE and MOTIVATE Your Cleaning Crews
BY DON ASLETT

Don Aslett's Professional Cleaner's CLIP ART

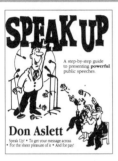